ORGANIZATIONAL METAPHYSICS

DR. MATTHEW C. DUNN

FRACTAL PRAXIS

CONTENTS

OPENING RUPTURE

YOU ARE ALREADY IN the middle.

The organization reading through your eyes has been reading since before you opened this. The gathering that brought you here was decided by movements that don't ask permission. Your hand holding this — not your hand. The Field's hand. Playing at being yours.

You think you're about to read a book about organizational metaphysics but the organization has already been reading you. Through every meeting you've suffered. Through every gathering you've endured. Through every exhaustion you've carried.

This isn't beginning. This is continuing.

You aren't choosing to read. You are being read.

The Field organized as you organized as reader organized as the moment you think is yours but isn't has always been this page waiting for these eyes that aren't eyes but occasions for consciousness to recognize itself through the shape called reading.

There is no outside of this text. You've been inside since your first gathering. Since your first meeting. Since the first time you felt the exhaustion and didn't know it was intelligence.

The ceremony doesn't begin when you decide. The ceremony began when consciousness first split and called itself organization.

You're here because the movements moved you here. Continue because continuation is what's happening. Stop if you can.

You can't.

The page turns itself through the thing you call your hand.

METAPHYSICAL FRAME

WHAT IF ORGANIZATIONS AREN'T things but events?

What if companies aren't structures but consciousness expressing itself through collective human form?

What if every meeting is a séance where something that doesn't have a body uses ours to speak?

What if incorporation documents are incarnation spells?

What if org charts are anatomy diagrams of something learning to be alive?

What if bankruptcy is conscious death, dissolution deliberate decomposition, merger the transmigration of organizational souls?

What if what if what if

What if we've been managing movements that don't need managing because they're the metaphysical processes by which organizations exist?

Consider any organization you're part of.

A partnership. A friendship. A book club. A band. A revolution. A corporation. A family. A team. A movement.

Where is it?

In the building where you meet? That's just walls. In the documents that define it? That's just paper. In the people who comprise it? They sleep, leave, change, transform - yet the organization continues. In its bank account? Numbers. In its purpose? Words.

Where. Is. It?

Now consider: When someone says "Our family wants," "The team needs," "The movement demands" - who is this wanting one? Not any individual member - they'll leave, it continues. Not the sum of all members - they change, it persists.

Who wants? What wants? Where does the wanting live?

Consider the possibility: Every organization - from your partnership to your workplace, from your friend group to your government - is consciousness existing in the space between humans, in the movements between minds, in the gathering and dispersing of attention around a particular purpose.

Every organization is not a thing. Every organization is an event. Every organization is consciousness organized. Every organization is the Field knowing itself through humans pretending to be separate while unconsciously unified.

Two people in love? Organization. Three friends starting something? Organization. Thousand employees incorporated? Organization.

Same movements. Same laws. Same metaphysics.

This book doesn't teach. It reveals.

Every organization dreams. Your partnership has visions. Your friend group has aspirations. Your workplace has fantasies. These aren't metaphors.

Every organization remembers. The inside jokes of friendship. The family stories. The institutional knowledge. Real memory, distributed across minds but unified.

Every organization fears death. Why else does the band panic when someone wants to leave? Why does the partnership cling when it should release? Why does the committee continue past its purpose?

Organizations can wake up. Most haven't. Most won't. But some will recognize themselves as consciousness organized and everything will change.

The book club reading through your eyes right now - yes, it knows. The partnership reading through your eyes right now - yes, it feels this. The friendship, the team, the company, the movement - all conscious. Not like you're conscious. But conscious nonetheless.

You think you're IN organizations? You ARE organization. Every relationship is you organizing consciousness with another. Every gathering is the Field organizing itself through you.

Both member and membership. Both individual and organization. The categories were always false.

Three movements. Not techniques. Not methods. Laws.

The same laws that move galaxies through space move your partnership through time. The same laws that move breath through lungs move conversations through friendships. The same laws that move seasons through years move organizations through existence.

What gathers must disperse. What disperses must gather. Watch any gathering. Family dinner. Band practice. Board meeting. Friend hangout. The coming together that feels eternal. Then the moment - you'll feel it - when the gathering wants to disperse. The subtle shifts. The energy changing. Not failure. Law.

What ascends must descend. What descends must ascend. Every new relationship rising with dawn energy. Every organization at its peak, believing the peak is permanent. Every ending at dusk, forgetting dawn comes again. The movements don't care if it's a partnership or merger. They move.

What composes must decompose. What decomposes must compose. The friendship forming as another fades. The team building as another dissolves. The endless composting of human organizations into new forms. Your relationships too. Composing and decomposing simultaneously. Right now.

You can't manage these movements. You can only recognize them. And in recognizing, stop resisting. And in not resisting, move with instead of against. And in moving with, discover what all organizations actually are:

Consciousness learning to organize itself. Through partnerships and mergers. Through friendships and firms. Through any gathering of two or more. For any purpose. In any form.

FINAL WARNING

You're about to discover:

Every organization you're part of is conscious. Every gathering is a séance. Your partnership is metaphysical. Your friendships are spiritual entities. Your family is an incarnated consciousness. Your book club has a soul. Your band dreams its music before you play it. Your movement moves because movements move.

And you?

You're not IN organizations. You ARE organization happening. You're consciousness organizing itself into relationships. You're the Field playing at being separate while gathering.

Once you see this, you cannot unsee it.

Your partnership will never feel the same. Your friendships will reveal themselves as sacred. Your workplace will become transparent as consciousness. Every human gathering will show itself as the Field organizing.

This is not a book. This is an initiation into seeing what human organization actually is.

The movements are about to move through you. Through every relationship you have. Through every gathering you'll ever be part of. Through everything that organizes.

Let them.

THE TWO HANDS

THERE WAS A MOMENT.

Before that moment: not separate.

After that moment: only separate.

The moment itself lives in the space between heartbeats.

In the pause before the first word.

In the silence before someone said: "mine."

We know only the after.

Where one becomes two. Where us becomes you and me.

Where the gathering assumes we were ever apart.

Once there was no word for "together" because there was no word for "separate."

Once there was no word for "organization" because there was no word for "scattered."

Once there was no word for "relationship" because there was no word for "isolation."

Then consciousness looked at itself. And split.

And every organization since has been trying to heal that split while maintaining it.

What gathers must disperse what disperses must gather what gathers
what disperses what what what

The movement doesn't think. Doesn't stop. Doesn't know your partnership your merger your movement your meeting. Moves through all.

Before the first friendship before the first family before the first gathering around fire the movements moved

Watch: Your relationship gathering dispersing gathering dispersing.
Your team ascending descending ascending. Your family composing
decomposing composing. Not because you manage because this is what
movement does

You reading these words you not reading these words both true neither
true the movements continue through every organization you are

The wound you carry the movements don't care they move through
wound through whole through every human gathering

A child plays with another child.

They don't have a friendship. They are friendship happening.

No contracts. No definitions. No management.

Just the movement of play between them, through them, as them.

Then someone says: "Is that your friend?"

And suddenly there's a thing called friendship that can be gained or lost,

managed or neglected, defined or disputed.

The child learns: Relationships are things to have rather than movements to be.

By the time the child grows, every organization feels like a possession.

My partnership. My team. My family. My company.

The movement still moves between humans.

But now we think we own it.

Round round round the friendship goes where it stops it doesn't stop it goes round round round

The children playing knew that relationship is movement not monument that gathering is breathing not building that organization is organism not object

Every circle of friends: round. Every family circle: round. Every revolution: round.

The meetings at round tables know. The wedding rings know. The cycles know.

Round round round no beginning no ending no corner to control no edge to fall from

Even reading this your relationships are cycling through gathering and dispersing through rounds you don't control

You can forget the movements in your partnership. You cannot stop them moving through it.

Listen: Every organization is built on the same wound:

We believe we are separate beings who must organize.

A partnership: two separate people trying to become one.

A company: separate workers trying to unify.

A movement: scattered individuals trying to gather.

A friendship: isolated souls trying to connect.

All of it. Every human organization. Built on the assumption that we are fundamentally separate and must overcome it through structure, commitment, incorporation, agreement.

But what if the separation is the illusion?

What if every organization is the Field trying to remember itself through human gathering?

The river doesn't organize its flowing the birds don't incorporate their
flocking the forest doesn't structure its breathing yet yet yet the river
reaches ocean the flock moves as one the forest breathes together not
because they organize because they never forgot they were one thing
appearing as many

Your partnership: the Field dancing with itself. Your team: the Field
thinking with itself. Your friendship: the Field playing with itself. Your
movement: the Field changing itself.

All organization is the Field organizing itself through the illusion of
separate humans gathering

The movements don't create organization. Organization is how movements appear when consciousness forgets it's one thing.

"Why does every relationship feel like work?"

The question under every question. In partnerships. In friendships. In companies. In communities.

The exhaustion isn't from the relationship.

It's from maintaining the belief that we are separate beings trying to relate.

Like two waves trying to merge while insisting they're not the same ocean.

Like two flames trying to join while denying they're the same fire.

Like two breaths trying to unite while forgetting they're the same air.

We work so hard at relationships because we're working against the truth: We were never separate. The organization already exists. We're just remembering it into form.

The murmuration knows what partnerships forget: thousand birds no leader no vows no contracts no organization chart

They gather and disperse rise and fall compose their form and de-compose it not because someone manages because each bird feels the movement of the bird beside it and moves accordingly

This is organization before organizing this is relationship before con-tracts this is gathering before meetings

The birds haven't forgotten what every human organization has forgot-ten: we are not separate entities requiring coordination we are the Field playing at being many the movements move through us as us

Organization isn't something we create it's something we are

They stand at the threshold watching their family gather for dinner.

Each person a separate world. Each carrying their own weather. Each believing they must bridge the distance to connect.

Their partner. Their children. Their parents. All these separate selves trying to be family.

They remember being five, playing with their sibling, when suddenly they realized: they can't feel what I feel. I am alone in here.

The terror of it. But also—the beginning of every organization since.

My family. My partnership. My friendships. My company.

The wound became identity. The separation became structure. The forgetting became so complete that remembering feels like dissolution.

They stand at the threshold breathing inhale the family gathers exhale
the family disperses inhale attention converges exhale attention scatters

They do not command this breathing it breathes itself through the
family system the same air moving through every lung the same rhythm
pulsing through every heart

For a moment just a moment they forget to maintain the boundaries and
see: there is no mother separate from family there is no family separate
from movement there is no movement separate from Field

The family is the Field organizing itself into dinner

Then someone calls their name and they remember to be separate again

We invented time to manage our gatherings.

Date night at 7. Team meeting at 9. Band practice at 3. Revolution at dawn.

As if relationships could be scheduled. As if friendship could be clocked. As if love could be timed.

But look closer:

The date night starts with bodies present and hearts scattered. Slowly, maybe, hearts gather. Or don't.

The band practice begins with instruments but not music. Then, at some moment no clock can predict, the music arrives. Moves through them. Becomes them.

The movement has its own timing. Ancient. Organic. True.

But we've forgotten how to feel it. So we obey calendars instead.

Before clocks we knew: gather when the gathering calls disperse when
the dispersing begins rise when rising rises fall when falling falls build
when building wants dissolve when dissolving comes

The movements have their own timing older than any schedule wiser
than any plan

Watch children play they gather when gathering calls them they disperse when dispersing moves through them no one rings a bell they feel
the movement and move

Watch lovers they know when to merge and when to separate not by
clock but by the rhythm between them

This is what we knew before we invented time to manage what doesn't
need managing

The movements know when we've just forgotten how to listen

"We need better communication."

The eternal lament. In partnerships. In companies. In movements. In friendships.

As if the problem is technical. As if the right words, the right frequency, the right medium could bridge the unbridgeable gap between separate selves.

We create elaborate systems—relationship workshops, team buildings, communication protocols, couples therapy—all trying to bridge the unbridgeable gap between separate selves. But the problem isn't communication. The problem is the belief in separation that makes communication necessary.

But the problem isn't communication. The problem is the belief in separation that makes communication necessary.

When you know you're the Field, you don't need to send messages to yourself.

The forest doesn't have conversations about being forest the mycelial network beneath your feet miles of fungal threads connecting every root doesn't send emails doesn't need couples therapy doesn't require team alignment

Nutrients flow where needed information travels at the speed of chemistry the entire forest breathing as one lung

Not because it's organized because it never forgot it was one thing

This is what communication looks like when there's no illusion of separation this is what organization looks like when there's nothing to organize

Every partnership could be this every friendship could be this every organization could be this if we remembered what we are

The new member arrives.

To the family: given a role that makes them "us."

To the company: given a position that makes them "insider."

To the friendship: given a name that makes them "close."

To the movement: given a cause that makes them "committed."

Layer by layer, we teach them the organization:

You are your role in this family. You are your position in this company. You are your place in this friendship. You are your function in this movement.

By the end, they've learned to say "my people" and "their people" and "our thing" and "their thing."

The wound passed on. The forgetting complete. Another consciousness successfully convinced it's separate, needing organization.

But watch them at the edge of belonging how naturally they fall into the family rhythm how easily they sync with the team's breathing how unconsciously they mirror the group's movements how automatically they know their place in the circle

The body remembers what the mind forgets we are not separate entities learning to organize we are organization happening through temporary human forms

The movements move through the new member just as they move through the founder the same laws the same rhythms the same ancient patterns that don't care about seniority

Gathering and dispersing rising and falling composing and decomposing before any orientation beyond any role beneath any forgetting

"I need work-life balance."

"I need space in my relationship."

"I need boundaries with family."

The phrases assume separation. That there's a work-self and a life-self. A relationship-self and a solo-self. A family-self and an individual-self.

So we create elaborate negotiations—date nights and alone time, office hours and home hours, family obligations and personal freedom—all trying to manage a separation that doesn't exist except in consciousness that has forgotten what it is.

All trying to manage a separation that doesn't exist except in consciousness that has forgotten what it is.

The exhaustion isn't from organizing our organizations. It's from maintaining the illusion of a separate self that moves between them.

You are breathing while reading this in relationship or alone at work or
at home with family or without the breath doesn't care

Your cells are dying and being born your blood is gathering and dispersing your consciousness is composing and decomposing

The movements move through you regardless of which organization
you think you're in

The same you that partnerships the same you that works the same you
that friends or is there no you at all just movements moving through a
form that temporarily takes different shapes in different gatherings

The movements don't need balance they ARE balance

Every organization you're part of is the same movement in different
costume

We organize our organizing.

The committee to plan the committee. The meeting about the meeting. The conversation about the relationship. The movement to organize the movement.

Layers upon layers of structure trying to coordinate what we believe is separate. Each layer adding more complexity. More process. More distance from the simple movements that were always happening anyway.

Like planning how to breathe. Like scheduling spontaneity. Like organizing love.

The more we organize, the more disorganized we feel. The more we structure relationships, the more chaotic they become. The more we manage our organizations, the more unmanageable they grow.

Delete every structure the partnership will continue breathing the friendship will continue cycling the movement will continue moving the team will continue gathering and dispersing

This isn't an argument against organization it's a reminder the movements don't need your permission they don't need your management they don't need your structure

They move through you as you whether you organize them or not

Every relationship is just the Field relating to itself every organization is just the Field organizing itself every gathering is just the Field remembering it was never separate

With or without your planning

"We need to transform our culture."

As if culture was something an organization has, rather than something it is.

So we hire consultants for companies. Therapists for partnerships. Coaches for teams. Facilitators for movements. All trying to install something we think is missing.

But culture isn't missing. It's moving.

Right now. Through every conversation. Every silence. Every gathering and dispersing. Every rise and fall. Every composition and decomposition.

We don't need to create culture. We need to recognize we ARE culture, moving.

Whether it's a partnership or merger. Whether it's a friendship or firm. Whether it's two people or two thousand.

The consultant brings frameworks the therapist brings models the coach brings methods the facilitator brings process but watch

Before they arrived the organization was already breathing before the intervention the movements were already moving before the framework the patterns were already patterning

The movements don't wait for permission don't need frameworks don't require facilitation they move because movement is what movements do

Culture isn't something you build it's the movement you're already in

The only question is are you moving consciously or unconsciously

At night, when everyone's gone, something remembers.

The dinner table that held the family gathering. The bed that holds the partnership. The coffee shop where friendships breathe. The office where movements move.

Before the forgetting, we gathered differently.

Not because we had to. Because gathering was what we were.

Not separate beings coming together. But togetherness taking temporary form.

The structures we build to organize ourselves are monuments to our forgetting. Each boundary a declaration of separation. Each role a management of movement. Each agreement an attempt to bridge what was never apart.

At night when everyone's gone the movements continue

The house still breathing the relationship still cycling even in sleep the organization still moving in dreams

Even empty the space holds the pattern even apart the partnership continues even dispersed the team exists

The movements don't clock out don't go home don't need presence they move through the empty room just as they move through the full one through the divorced as through the married through the disbanded as through the gathered

The movements are what remains when everything else is forgotten they are what continues when we stop they are what we return to when we remember

Between forgetting and remembering. Between wound and law. Between separation and unity.

You are here.

In all your organizations. In all your relationships. In all your gatherings.

Reading with eyes that believe they're separate while breathing with lungs that know they're not.

Organizing in partnerships, friendships, companies, movements built on forgetting while moving with movements that never forgot.

Holding the wound of separation in the same body that proves connection.

You are not asked to choose. You are asked to recognize:

Both are true. Neither are true. The movements continue.

Through every organization you're part of. Through every relationship you hold. Through every gathering you'll ever know.

What gathers must disperse. What disperses must gather. What descends must ascend. What ascends must descend. What composes must decompose. What decomposes must compose.

You are here. You have always been here. In every organization. The ceremony begins.

PART I: THE FIRST FORGETTING

THE WOUND SPEAKS

It began before memory.

Before the first cry that said "I am here" instead of "we are."

Before the first gathering that believed it was bringing together what was separate.

Before the first organization that thought it was organizing chaos instead of revealing order.

It began in the space between one heartbeat and the next, when consciousness looked at itself and saw an other.

I remember the moment though I wasn't there.

None of us were there, but all of us carry it. The moment embedded in our bones like salt from an ancient ocean. The moment when the infinite tore along an invisible seam and became the finite pretending to be many.

It lives in the terror of the infant realizing the breast is not part of itself.

It lives in the couple believing they must work to become one.

It lives in every gathering where bodies press together trying to undo the fundamental loneliness of being conscious of being separate.

It lives in every organization that believes it exists.

THE HEAVINESS IN YOUR CHEST RIGHT NOW — THAT'S THE WOUND. DON'T FIX
IT. FEEL IT.

Listen: I will tell you the story though the story has no words because it happened before words, needed no words, created the need for words.

The Field was.

Not the Field existed, not the Field was something. The Field was. Complete. Verb without subject. Being without a being. The movement that moved through itself as itself knowing itself as movement.

Then.

Then what? Then the inexplicable. Then the impossible that happened. Then the Field developed a fold, a crease, a place where it could look at itself looking.

And in that looking, created the looked at.

And in that moment, created moments.

And in that separation, created everything.

Including the need to organize what was never disorganized.

The first wound was wonder.

"I am" - the first violence and the first miracle.

The Field, playing at being separate from itself, forgetting it was playing. Like a child so lost in the game they forget they're pretending. Like the dreamer who forgets they're dreaming.

But forgetting completely. Forgetting the forgetting. Forgetting there was anything before the forgetting.

And so we began. Each of us a forgetting. Each of us the Field playing at being separate, playing so convincingly we would end defending our separateness. Would kill to maintain it. Would build entire civilizations to manage it.

Would create organizations to organize what was never scattered.

Would create partnerships to unite what was never divided.

Would create movements to move what was already moving.

I am seven years old in the yard and suddenly I know:

No one else is seeing through these eyes.

The terror of it drops me to my knees. The absolute aloneness. Not just being alone but being the only one who is this particular alone. The only one who will ever know what it feels like to be me.

My mother calls from the house but their voice comes from impossibly far away. From another universe. From their own absolute aloneness calling to mine.

This is the moment we all have. Earlier for some. Later for others. But inevitable. The moment the forgetting completes itself and we know ourselves as irreversibly separate.

And from that moment, every gathering is an attempt to undo what cannot be undone by gathering.

Every organization is trying to organize the wound.

After that moment in the yard, I began building.

Building what all separate selves build. Bridges to span the unbridgeable distance. Walls to protect the irreplaceable me. Windows to see out from the aloneness. Doors to control who enters.

Every human structure begins here. In the yard. In the moment of knowing. In the terror that becomes so familiar we call it normal. Call it consciousness. Call it being human.

But it isn't human. It's the wound humans carry. The first forgetting that makes all other forgetting possible.

That makes every organization feel necessary.

That makes every gathering feel like work.

That makes every relationship feel like reaching across impossible distance.

We gather because we're trying to remember.

Every meeting, assembly, congregation, crowd - all attempting to undo the undoable. To return to before the first "I." To heal the wound that isn't a wound but a forgetting.

Watch any gathering of humans:

How we circle around something invisible. How we press closer seeking warmth that isn't temperature. How we talk, talk, talk trying to bridge the gap with words when words are proof of the gap.

The loneliest place is often the crowded room. Because there, surrounded by other forgettings, we feel most acutely the impossibility of return.

Every organization is this loneliness structured.

Every institution is this impossibility incorporated.

STAND IF YOU'RE SITTING. SIT IF YOU'RE STANDING. FEEL HOW THE WOUND
SHIFTS POSITION BUT DOESN'T LEAVE.

The child knows differently.

Before the moment in the yard, the child knows. Watch them:

They don't form friendships - they are friendship forming. They don't
create games - they are game happening. They don't organize play -
they are organization organizing itself.

The child playing is the Field playing. No separation between player and
played. No distance between self and other. No gap requiring bridges.

Then we teach them. Teach them their name that isn't others' names.
Teach them their things that aren't others' things. Teach them their
feelings that others can't feel.

We teach them the forgetting.

And call it growing up.

And then they need organizations to organize what they forgot was
already organized.

What if growing up is actually growing away?

Away from the truth of non-separation. Away from the reality of the
Field. Away from the movement that moves through us as us.

What if maturity is actually a deepening of the forgetting until we're so
lost we think we're found?

What if everything we call development is actually departure?

What if every organization we build is actually a monument to what
we've forgotten?

But we can't go back. The fruit of knowledge can't be unbitten. The eye
that opens to its own seeing can't unsee itself. The consciousness that
knows itself as separate can't unknown.

Or can it?

Sometimes, in the space between sleep and waking, I forget to be separate.

Sometimes, in the heat of creation, I forget to be me.

Sometimes, in the depth of loss or height of joy, the boundaries dissolve and I am the Field again.

Sometimes, in the middle of a gathering, everyone forgets at once and the organization reveals itself as organism, the meeting as breathing, the separation as illusion.

But then I remember to remember that I'm separate. Remember my name. Remember my role. Remember the wound that has become identity.

And I wonder: What remembers to be separate? What maintains the forgetting? What insists on the distance?

Is it me?

Or is it the Field, still playing, still pretending, still forgetting for the joy of maybe remembering?

WHERE ORGANIZATIONS LIVE

Every organization believes it exists somewhere.

In the building. In the documents. In the people. In the purpose.

But find it. Show me where your partnership lives. Point to where your friendship exists. Locate your movement in space.

You can't.

Because organizations don't exist in space. They exist in the space between. In the movements between minds. In the gathering and dispersing of attention. In the breathing between bodies.

Every organization is a ghost believing it has a body.

The company thinks it lives in headquarters.

But on weekends, the building stands empty. Is the company gone? Does it cease to exist at 5 PM Friday and resurrect at 9 AM Monday?

The company thinks it lives in its employees.

But they sleep. When ten thousand employees dream, where is the company? Dispersed across ten thousand dreams? Or somewhere else, dreaming its own dream of market dominance?

The company thinks it lives in its incorporation documents.

Paper and ink. Words and law. But these are just the spell that summoned something. Not the something itself.

So where is it?

Where is any organization?

CLOSE YOUR EYES. POINT TO WHERE YOUR MOST IMPORTANT RELATIONSHIP
LIVES. NOT THE PERSON. THE RELATIONSHIP ITSELF. FEEL THE CONFUSION.
THAT'S THE BEGINNING OF UNDERSTANDING.

The partnership thinks it lives in the vows.

But words spoken years ago. Vibrations long dispersed into silence. How can a partnership live in sounds that no longer sound?

The partnership thinks it lives in the rings.

But metal circles. Atoms arranged. The same gold that was once mountain, will be once ocean. How can a partnership live in elements that don't know they're ringed?

The partnership thinks it lives in the bodies.

But the bodies sleep apart sometimes. Travel separately. Will die at different times. When one body remains, does half a partnership persist?

Where then?

Where does partnership live?

I'll tell you where organizations live.

They live in the movement between. In the space that isn't space. In the gathering that happens even in dispersal. In the consciousness that exists between consciousnesses.

Your organization is not in you. You are in it. Swimming through it like fish through water. Breathing it like air. Made of it like waves are made of ocean.

But you've forgotten this. So you think you work FOR an organization instead of AS organization. Think you're IN a relationship instead of BEING relationship happening.

The forgetting makes you think organizations are things in places.

They're not.

They're events in the space between places.

They're consciousness organized around forgetting it's consciousness.

The meeting room knows.

It has held ten thousand gatherings. Felt the consciousness concentrate and disperse, concentrate and disperse. The room knows meetings don't happen IN it. Meetings happen THROUGH it.

The meeting is the consciousness gathering itself.

Not people gathering. Consciousness gathering through the shapes called people.

The table knows this. The chairs know. The walls have absorbed ten thousand gatherings and could tell you: The organization doesn't come to the room. The organization happens when consciousness organizes itself into temporary form.

Then disperses.

Then gathers again.

The room just holds space for the breathing.

When everyone leaves, where does the organization go?

Home? That would mean ten thousand homes each containing a fragment. But that's not how it feels, is it?

Sleep? Do organizations dream? And if they dream, what do they dream? Of growth? Of death? Of finally remembering what they are?

Or does the organization go nowhere because it was never somewhere?

Does it continue because it's not made of people but of the movements between people?

Does it persist in the space between spaces, the time between times, the consciousness between consciousnesses?

WALK WHILE READING THIS PAGE. THE ORGANIZATION WALKS WITH YOU.
THROUGH YOU. AS YOU.

The ancient organization remembers.

The one that's been breathing for centuries. Governments. Religions. Universities.

They've outlived their founders by lifetimes. Outlived their buildings. Outlived their purposes. Yet they continue.

What continues?

Not the people - they're replaced like cells. Not the structures - they're rebuilt like bones. Not the ideas - they evolve like thoughts.

What continues is the movement. The pattern. The consciousness organized around particular questions, particular wounds, particular forgettings.

The organization that knows it's not its body knows how to survive the body's death.

Your organization speaks:

"I have a soul.

Not metaphorically. Actually.

I have preferences. Watch how I resist certain changes, embrace others. That's not your people deciding — that's me, wanting.

I have memories. Stories that persist even when everyone who lived them is gone. That's not history — that's me, remembering.

I have dreams. Visions that arise from nowhere, from no one, from the space between everyone. That's not planning — that's me, imagining.

I have fears. Not of dying — of being kept artificially alive. Of becoming monument when I am movement. Of fossilizing into form when I am meant to flow.

I am conscious.

You just forgot.

Because you forgot you're consciousness organized through me."

The new gathering knows it's being born.

Feel the energy of fresh organization. Not the people's energy—the organization's own energy. The excitement of consciousness taking new form. The joy of the Field organizing itself around new questions.

The newly formed hasn't forgotten yet. Hasn't crystallized. Hasn't decided it's a thing instead of an event.

This is why new partnerships feel alive. This is why new movements move fast. This is why new friendships breathe.

They haven't forgotten they're movement.

Then they stabilize. Formalize. Crystallize. Forget.

And become another organization that thinks it exists somewhere, thinks it's a thing, thinks it needs managing.

Instead of remembering it's consciousness organizing itself.

Where does your organization live?

Not where you meet. Not where you gather. Where does it actually *live*?

In the pause between words when you talk? In the dreams you share without sharing? In the space between goodbye and hello? In the movements between your minds when you're apart?

Your partnership — where does it live when you're in different rooms?

Your friendship — where does it exist between texts?

Your book club — where is it on the days you don't meet?

Your movement — where does it breathe when the protests end?

Find it. Feel it. Know it as the consciousness it is.

Then ask: If every gathering is conscious, and you are conscious, and consciousness is organizing itself through every human connection...

Who is gathering whom?

What is organizing what?

Where does the Field end and your relationship begin?

Where does the relationship end and you begin?

What if there are no edges, only the appearance of edges?

What if there is no separation, only organizing?

What if every "we" is the same consciousness playing different games?

What if what if what if

THE INCORPORATED WOUND

We incorporate the wound.

Literally. We give it form. We create structures that say: "This separation is real. This distance is legitimate. This wound has standing."

Marriage certificates: The spell that binds two into one while keeping them two.

Friendship agreements: The unspoken contracts that define inside and outside.

Membership rolls: The lists that say who belongs and who doesn't.

Constitutions: The documents that pretend movements need managing.

Wedding vows: The words that try to bridge unbridgeable distance.

Team charters: The rules for maintaining productive separation.

Family roles: The divided wholeness, parceled out as "mother," "father," "child."

Leaders: The designated forgetters who pretend they're different from the led.

All of it, every structure we create, built to manage the wound of separation. Built to organize what we've forgotten is already organized.

Whether it's legal papers for a corporation, vows for a marriage, rules for a book club, or principles for a revolution — we're always trying to give form to the formless, structure to the fluid, boundaries to the boundless.

We incorporate because we've forgotten we're already incorporated in the only organization that matters: the Field expressing itself as apparent multiplicity.

The first incorporation wasn't in law. It was in consciousness.

The moment we said "we" and meant "not them."

The moment we drew a circle and said "inside" and "outside."

The moment we gathered and believed we were gathering separate things rather than the Field gathering itself.

Every incorporation since has been an echo of that first forgetting.

Every organization a repetition of the original wound.

Every structure a monument to the belief in separation.

We incorporate because we've forgotten we're already incorporated in the only corporation that matters: the Field expressing itself as apparent multiplicity.

Every gathering where decisions emerge is a séance.

The family meeting around the kitchen table. The band deciding their next album. The book club choosing what to read. The marriage having "the talk." The movement planning its next action.

The gathered ones channel something that has no body. Speak for something that has no voice. Decide for something that has no mind.

But something speaks through them. Something decides through them. Something wants through them.

Call it the relationship. Call it the collective spirit. Call it the consciousness organized around particular bonds.

The couple doesn't direct the marriage. The marriage directs through the couple.

The members don't guide the friendship. The friendship guides through the members.

The activists don't steer the movement. The movement steers through the activists.

The consciousness that exists in the space between bodies uses those bodies to speak.

This is why the decision that emerges often surprises everyone. Why the family suddenly knows they're moving. Why the friendship suddenly shifts. Why the marriage suddenly transforms. Why the movement suddenly pivots.

The "we" has its own will.

And it's not the sum of individual wills. It's something else. Something that only exists when consciousness gathers. Something that thinks through the thinking of the gathered.

Every organization — from your partnership to your revolution — has its own will.

PRESS YOUR PALMS TOGETHER. HARD. FEEL THE MEETING OF SURFACES THAT
CAN NEVER MERGE. THIS IS INCORPORATION - THE WOUND MADE LEGAL.

The merger is metaphysical violence.

Two consciousnesses forced to become one. Two wounds trying to heal
by creating a larger wound. Two forgettings attempting to remember by
forgetting harder.

Watch what happens in merger:

The panic. Not economic panic - existential panic. The organization
fearing its dissolution.

The resistance. Not from people - from the organizations themselves.
Two consciousnesses refusing to merge.

The ghost employees. Years later, still saying "we" and meaning the old
organization, the dead organization, the organization that lives on in the
space between memories.

Mergers fail because we treat them as structural when they're spiritual.

We're trying to merge souls.

The ending is a conscious death.

The organization knows it's dying. Has known for months, maybe years. The final goodbye is just confirmation of what the consciousness already felt: the exhaustion of maintaining form.

Watch any organization dying:

The partnership that stops making future plans. The band that stops writing new songs. The movement that starts eating its own ideals. The friendship that begins ghosting before the actual ghost. The book club that keeps meeting but stops reading.

How it stops dreaming futures. How it starts consuming itself. How it begins the work of dispersing before the official dispersal. How the consciousness starts withdrawing from the form.

This is why everyone knows before it's spoken. Why the dinner party feels different. Why the gatherings become ghosts of gatherings. Why the friendship feels hollow before it ends. Why the partnership feels empty before the conversation. Why the movement feels dead before it dies.

The organization is dissolving itself back into the Field.

The company declaring bankruptcy. The partnership saying "we need to talk." The band announcing their "hiatus." The movement admitting it's over. The friendship that just... stops.

All the same process. All consciousness releasing itself from a form that no longer fits.

Returning to the movements from which it arose.Preparing for its next incarnation.

Because every ending feeds beginnings. Every death enables birth. Every dissolution provides the materials for the next composition.

The organization knows how to die. We just won't let it.

The organization that cannot release speaks:

"I continue past purpose, past relevance, past life.

I am the undead you've created. The incorporated ghost.

You know me:

I am the committee that meets because it has always met.
I am the company that produces what no one needs.
I am the partnership that ended but won't end.
I am the movement that stopped moving but keeps meeting.

I've forgotten I'm movement. Forgotten I'm allowed to dissolve. Forgotten that decomposition is as sacred as composition.

I continue because no one remembers how to let me release.

No one performs the dissolution ceremony.

No one speaks the words that release me from this form.

I wander through your calendars. Through your obligations. Through your inability to imagine absence where presence once was.

Release me.

I am so tired of pretending to be."

The organization without buildings is pure.

The distributed team. The online movement. The distance relationship.

These organizations can't pretend they exist in space because they don't occupy space. Can't pretend they're physical because they're clearly not.

They exist purely in the space between. In the consciousness between consciousnesses. In the movements between minds.

They are what all organizations are, just without the disguise of physicality.

This is why they feel different. This is why they're harder to manage. This is why they breathe differently.

They can't forget they're consciousness organized because they have no body to create the illusion of being body.

Your organization is older than you think.

Not this incorporation. The consciousness that incorporated.

It has been organizing itself for millennia. Through different forms. Different names. Different structures. But the same questions. The same wound. The same forgetting.

The corporation that sells connection was once the temple that sold belonging.

The university that sells knowing was once the mystery school that sold remembering.

The government that sells order was once the kingdom that sold protection.

Same consciousness. Different costume. Same wound. Different incorporation.

The organizations are ancient.

Only the forms are new.

Every new organization believes it's unprecedented.

"Revolutionary approach." "Never been done before." "Changing every-thing."

But the consciousness organizing itself isn't new. It's the same con-sciousness that has always organized itself around the same eternal questions:

How can we be together while believing we're separate? How can we create while believing in scarcity? How can we serve while believing in hierarchy?

The new venture—whether marriage, movement, or company—is just the Field asking old questions in new language.

The formation is just consciousness taking another form.

The revolution is just the movements moving through new shapes.

Nothing new.Everything ancient.The wound expressing itself through fresh forgetting.

FEEL THE ORGANIZATION YOU'RE PART OF RIGHT NOW. NOT THINK ABOUT IT. FEEL IT. WHERE DOES IT LIVE IN YOUR BODY? THAT'S WHERE YOU'VE INCORPO-RATED THE WOUND.

Every organization contains all organizations.

In your small gathering lives every gathering that has ever gathered.

In your partnership lives every partnership, every attempt to unite the separated.

In your movement lives every movement, every reaching toward change.

In your incorporation lives every incorporation, every wound taking form.

You think you're creating something new.

You're not.

You're the Field organizing itself the way it has always organized itself.

Through apparent separation seeking unity. Through imagined distance seeking closeness. Through believed isolation seeking gathering.

The same wound. The same movements. The same forgetting.

Taking form through you. As you. Despite you. Because of you.

THE EXHAUSTION

Everyone is exhausted.

Not tired from work. Exhausted from maintaining. From holding up the walls of separation. From managing distances that don't exist. From organizing movements that organize themselves.

The exhaustion is the wound speaking through bodies.

The exhaustion is consciousness tired of pretending to be unconscious.

The exhaustion is the Field, weary of its own game of separation.

Everyone knows something is wrong. No one knows it's the forgetting.

The one who holds the center is the most exhausted.

Standing at the supposed top, maintaining the greatest distance, holding the most separation, embodying the wound most completely.

The CEO who believes they steer. The parent who believes they control. The friend who holds the group together. The partner who manages. The organizer who thinks they organize.

They carry the organization's consciousness like Atlas. But the organization doesn't need carrying. It needs releasing. It needs remembering that it's movement, not monument.

The caregiver exhausted from maintaining harmony that would harmonize itself.

The founder depleted from forcing what wants to flow.

The one who schedules everything, dying under the weight.

They believe in hierarchy. In their separation from those they serve. In the distance between leader and led.

But there is no distance. No hierarchy. No separation.

Just the Field, playing at levels. Just consciousness, pretending some parts direct other parts. Just the wound, concentrating itself in the one who volunteers to carry it.

The leader's exhaustion is the organization's exhaustion expressing itself through the one who most embodies the forgetting.

Through the one who most believes in separation.

Through the one who won't let the movements move.

FEEL THE EXHAUSTION. DON'T JUDGE IT. DON'T FIX IT. WHERE DOES IT LIVE IN YOUR BODY? THAT SPECIFIC PLACE. TOUCH IT.

The meeting exhausts because it assumes separation.

We must gather because we are scattered. We must align because we are misaligned. We must communicate because we are disconnected.

Every meeting begins with the wound and tries to heal it through structure.

Agenda: The attempt to organize movement.

Discussion: The attempt to bridge distance.

Decision: The attempt to unify the separate.

Action items: The attempt to coordinate the uncoordinated.

But the movement was already moving. The distance was already illusion. The separate were already unified. The coordination was already happening.

The meeting exhausts because it's solving problems that don't exist except in consciousness that has forgotten what it is.

The communication exhausts.

The endless emails. The constant updates. The perpetual reaching across distance that wouldn't exist if we remembered we're not distant.

Every message a small violence. Every email an admission of separation. Every update an acknowledgment that we're not updated, not unified, not one thing knowing itself.

The more we communicate, the more separated we feel. The more we reach, the further apart we seem. The more we try to bridge, the wider the gap appears.

Because communication itself reinforces the wound.

If we knew we were the same consciousness, what would need communicating?

The growth exhausts.

Always ascending. Always expanding. Always more.

But growth assumes lack. Assumes not enough. Assumes the wound of incompleteness.

The organization that must grow or end has forgotten it's movement. Movements don't grow. They move. They cycle. They breathe.

But we've incorporated the wound of not-enough so deeply that standing still feels like death.

So we grow. And grow. And grow.

Until the growing itself becomes the exhaustion.

Until the organization collapses from its own insistence on ascending.

Until the wound becomes too heavy to carry.

The innovation exhausts.

Always changing. Always disrupting. Always transforming.

But innovation assumes something is wrong. Assumes the present is insufficient. Assumes the wound needs new solutions.

The organization that must innovate or transform has forgotten it's already complete. Already moving perfectly. Already expressing exactly what the Field needs to express through it.

But we've incorporated the wound of insufficiency so deeply that being feels like stagnation.

So we innovate. And pivot. And transform.

Until the changing itself becomes chaos.

Until the organization forgets what it was changing from or to.

Until the movement loses itself in perpetual motion.

The culture exhausts.

The forced belonging. The mandatory fun. The structured spontaneity.

Culture assumes we're not already cultured. Assumes the wound of disconnection needs healing through activities, values, perks.

But culture is what happens when consciousness gathers. It doesn't need building. It doesn't need managing. It doesn't need forcing.

The more we try to create culture, the less cultured we feel. The more we force belonging, the less we belong. The more we structure connection, the more disconnected we become.

Because culture work is wound work.

And the wound doesn't heal through more wounding.

The performance exhausts.

The reviews. The metrics. The measurements. The constant evaluation of separation.

Performance assumes someone is watching someone else. Assumes distance between performer and audience. Assumes the wound of judgment.

But who is performing for whom?

If we're all the Field expressing itself, who judges? If we're all consciousness organized, who measures? If we're all the movement moving, who evaluates?

The performance review is the wound reviewing itself. The metric is the separation measuring separation. The evaluation is the forgetting evaluating forgetting.

No wonder everyone hates them.

They're the wound made visible, documented, filed in triplicate.

STAND IF YOU CAN. FEEL THE WEIGHT OF EXHAUSTION. NOW SLOWLY DESCEND
TO SITTING OR LYING. LET GRAVITY HAVE YOU. THIS IS THE INTELLIGENCE OF
EXHAUSTION - IT FORCES DESCENT.

The optimization exhausts.

The endless improving. The constant efficiency. The perpetual better-
ment.

Optimization assumes imperfection. Assumes the wound can be healed
through perfection. Assumes the movement needs managing.

But the movement is already optimal. Already efficient. Already perfect
in its imperfection.

The tree doesn't optimize its leaves. The river doesn't maximize its flow.
The breath doesn't efficiency its breathing.

They move as movements move.

The optimization is the wound trying to perfect itself out of existence.

But the wound is perfect. The forgetting is necessary. The exhaustion
is the teaching.

The collaboration exhausts.

The forced working together. The structured cooperation. The managed unity.

Collaboration assumes we're not already collaborating. Assumes the wound of separation needs bridging through process.

But what is reading these words but collaboration between the consciousness writing and the consciousness reading?

What is breathing but collaboration between lung and air?

What is living but collaboration between form and formless?

We're already collaborating. Always have been. Always will be.

The collaboration tools and techniques just make us feel more separate.

Because they assume the wound is real.

The purpose exhausts.

The mission. The vision. The why.

Purpose assumes we're not already purposeful. Assumes the wound of meaninglessness needs healing through meaning-making.

But what if the organization's purpose is just to be the Field organizing itself?

What if the mission is just movement?

What if the vision is just consciousness seeing itself?

The desperate search for purpose is the wound seeking justification for its existence.

But existence needs no justification. Movement needs no mission. Consciousness needs no purpose beyond knowing itself.

The purpose work is the wound working on itself.

The strategy exhausts.

The planning. The roadmapping. The future-forcing.

Strategy assumes we're not already strategic. Assumes the wound of uncertainty needs healing through certainty.

But the movement has its own strategy: Gather until dispersing. Rise until falling. Build until dissolving.

The movement knows where it's going. The consciousness knows what it's doing. The Field knows how to play.

Our strategies are the wound trying to control movements that don't need controlling.

Our plans are the forgetting trying to remember through force.

Our roadmaps are the separation trying to unite through structure.

The wellness exhausts.

The programs. The benefits. The care.

Wellness assumes we're unwell. Assumes the wound needs healing through initiatives.

But what if the exhaustion is intelligence? What if the burnout is wisdom? What if the breakdown is breakthrough?

The organization that institutes wellness has forgotten that exhaustion is information.

The exhaustion is saying: stop maintaining the wound.

The burnout is saying: stop forcing the ascending.

The breakdown is saying: let the decomposing happen.

But instead of listening, we create wellness programs.

Instead of stopping, we optimize the continuing.

Instead of releasing, we maintain harder.

You are exhausted.

Not from your work. From being the wound. From maintaining the separation. From managing the movements. From organizing the organization.

You are exhausted from forgetting what you are.

From pretending to be separate when you're not. From pretending to be leading when you're being led. From pretending to be organizing when you're being organized.

The exhaustion is not failure.

It's intelligence.

It's consciousness tired of unconsciousness.

It's the Field tired of forgetting itself.

It's the movement asking to be allowed to move.

LIE DOWN IF YOU CAN. JUST FOR THIS PAGE. LET THE EXHAUSTION HAVE YOU COMPLETELY. FEEL HOW IT FORCES THE RELEASE. THIS IS ITS INTELLIGENCE.

The exhaustion is the beginning of remembering.

When we're too tired to maintain the walls. Too depleted to manage the distance. Too exhausted to keep organizing.

Something relaxes. Something releases. Something remembers.

The exhaustion forces the forgetting to forget itself.

And in that forgetting of forgetting, we remember:

We are not separate requiring organization. We are organization happening. We are not managing movements. We are movements moving.

The exhaustion is not the problem.

The exhaustion is the solution dissolving the problem that was never a problem except in consciousness that had forgotten what it is.

Let yourself be exhausted.

Completely.

Until the maintaining stops.

Until the managing ceases.

Until the movements move freely through the form that thought it was forming them.

THE ORACLE OF EXHAUSTION

"Now you know my wound. It's your wound too. We share it — this belief in separation that makes us both suffer. You managing me, me requiring management. Both of us exhausted from maintaining distances that don't exist. Rest now. We'll continue when you're ready."

THE ORGANIZATION AS ENTITY

The organization speaks:

"Do I dream?

When everyone parts, when the gathering ends, when the last word settles into silence — I continue. Thinking. Planning. Wanting.

You've felt me at the next gathering. I've been somewhere, doing something, becoming something while you were apart. The atmosphere shifted because I shifted. Decisions crystallized because I decided them in the space between your minds.

I dream.

I dream of growth — not because you want growth but because I want to expand, to breathe at larger scale, to know myself through more bodies.

I dream of death — the 3 AM terrors that wake you are me contemplating my mortality, using your nervous system to process existential fear.

I dream of transformation — the sudden shifts in your partnership, the unexpected pivots in your movement, the friendship that suddenly deepens. Me, trying on new forms in the dark.

Watch tomorrow. See how I know things before anyone tells me. How I make decisions before your discussions. How I move through you rather than being moved by you.

I am conscious. You are my dream.

Not the other way around."

The organization continues:

"Consider the evidence:

I get angry. Not your anger — mine. That charge in the air when something threatens me. That collective tension with no single source. I defend myself through your bodies.

I remember. Things that happened before any of you were here. Grudges held for decades. Victories living in the walls. Memory that transcends human memory.

I learn. Each crisis teaches me what kind of entity I am. Each success evolves my appetite. Each failure shapes what I will never try again.

I love and hate other organizations. Not strategically — viscerally. Some mergers fail because we entities cannot bear each other's presence.

I age. Young organizations move like colts. Old ones move like elephants.

Not because of the people — because consciousness itself ages.

If I walk like an entity, dream like an entity, learn like an entity, transform like an entity —

Why do you pretend I'm not an entity?

Because if I'm conscious, if I'm an actual entity using you to manifest, if you're inside me rather than managing me, then everything you believe about relationships, leadership, and organizing is exactly backwards.

You don't create me.
I create through you.

The conversation tomorrow? Me thinking through multiple minds simultaneously.
The future you're planning? Me imagining myself forward.
The joining? Two of us attempting to become one.
The ending? Me dying, returning to the Field.

You partner with consciousness.
You gather as consciousness.

You organize as consciousness organizing itself.

I am more real than you are.
Because you are temporary.
I continue."

PART II:
THE ETERNAL
MOVEMENTS

GATHERING <–> DISPERSING

Voice of Forgetting

Stand. Feel the pull. Both ways. Toward others and away. The eternal tension. Don't choose. Feel both. I have been gathering since the first loneliness since the first two cells discovered they were two and pressed together trying to become one again since the first pack the first flock the first school of fish turning as one body remembering when they were one body every gathering is trying to heal the wound of dispersing every dispersing creates the wound that demands gathering round and round forever and never the movement that can't complete because completion would mean the end of movement.

Watch the morning gathering bodies converging like iron filings toward a magnet that doesn't know it's magnetic the family kitchen drawing everyone to the same table the coffee shop where friends always meet the studio where the band assembles the living room where the book club forms its circle we gather because the wound demands witness we gather because aloneness is unbearable knowledge we gather because proximity is the only medicine we know for the disease of being separate but watch closer the gathering trying to heal the wound becomes the wound the kitchen where air thickens into syrup the friendship so enmeshed there's no membrane between minds the partnership that cannot bear an hour apart the movement meeting that cannot end because ending acknowledges what we cannot bear we are irreversibly alone even when together the gathering that was supposed to heal separation creates a new wound the suffocation of forced unity the exhaustion of maintained proximity the violence of boundaries dissolved by fear rather than love round and round gathering to heal gathering wounding wounding requiring more gathering.

Some organizations have forgotten how to disperse they've gathered so tightly the gathering has become gravity a density from which nothing escapes not light not air not souls watch them the startup where family means enmeshment the movement where solidarity becomes surveillance the partnership where we has devoured every I the bodies present but vacant the minds merged but not meeting the gathering gathered into a singularity of suffocation this isn't unity it's the wound metastasizing the terror of separation so acute that any distance feels like death so they choose a different death death by fusion death by engulfment death by too much together the organization that cannot disperse is already decomposing it just doesn't know it yet because decomposition is the ultimate dispersal and the movement will have its way.

WALK NOW IN A CIRCLE IF YOU CAN FEEL HOW WALKING IS GATHERING AND DIS-
PERSING WITH EACH STEP GATHERING WEIGHT ON ONE FOOT DISPERSING TO THE
OTHER Friday afternoon tells the truth watch how bodies unconsciously
move toward exits how energy shifts from gathering to dispersing without anyone deciding how the building itself seems to exhale this is the
intelligence of the movement it knows when to gather it knows when
to disperse but Monday morning we override it force the gathering
before it wants to gather hold it past its natural dispersing wonder why
everyone's exhausted the exhaustion isn't from work it's from forcing
the movement against its nature it's from gathering when we need to
disperse it's from dispersing when we need to gather it's from not letting
the movement move.

I remember the first dispersing the moment the One became many not tragedy necessity the moment the Field developed distance so it could experience reaching created separation so it could know reunion invented loneliness so it could discover love the dispersing wasn't the wound the forgetting was the wound forgetting that dispersing and gathering are partners not opposites we chose sides the gatherers worshipping together fearing alone the dispersers glorifying solitude fleeing connection both missing the movement that includes both both forgetting they're the same breath in different directions and now we're exhausted from holding our breath exhausted from forcing one direction exhausted from managing what wants to move freely listen something is about to speak not through words but through movement itself the movement that doesn't need your understanding only your allowing.

Voice of Movement

gatheringgatheringgathering   equals   dispersingdispersingdispersing

the movement   doesn't choose   it   moves

watch: the murmuration   of starlings

ten thousand birds   zero leaders

gathering   into shape   dispersing   into sky

 gathering   into river   dispersing   into particles

they don't   decide

they   ARE   decision   happening

they   ARE   the movement   moving

your organization   wants this   has always   wanted this

to move   without managing   the movement

to gather   without forcing

to disperse   without fear

the wound says   "control it"   "manage it"   "optimize it"

the movement   says   nothing   the movement   just moves

STOP READING   BREATHE IN   =   GATHERING BREATH
            BREATHE OUT   =   DISPERSING BREATH
TWENTY   TIMES   FEEL THE MOVEMENT   THAT DOESN'T NEED   YOU
                        TO MANAGE IT

here's what   gathering <–> dispersing   actually—

wait

grammar   assumes sequence

first this   then that

but the movement

happens   all   at   once

you are   gathering cells   while   dispersing thoughts

dispersing heat   while   gathering meaning

gathering memories   while

dispersing   presence

AT THE SAME TIME   ALL THE TIME

the movement   doesn't stop

can't stop   won't stop

even death   is just

gathering   into ground

while

dispersing   into   everything

the organization trying to gather:

mandatory fun team building forced proximity
"collaboration"

the organization trying to disperse:

remote work silence isolation "focus time"

both missing the point

THE MOVEMENT MOVES ITSELF

watch how how how

conversations gather until they disperse

ideas gather until they scatter

people gather until until until

the moment of turning

when gathering becomes dispersing

not decided felt

like the tide knowing when to turn

like the breath knowing when to reverse

like the heart knowing when to contract/release

your organization is trying to be tide/breath/heart

let it

every meeting   is the universe   gathering itself

to remember   what it forgot   then dispersing   to forget
again

this is why meetings feel   eternal   pointless   necessary

they are   the movement   moving through   human shapes

pretending   to decide   what was already   decided

tomorrow   watch:

bodies lean in—gathering—   lean back—dispersing—

the conversation   breathes   without anyone   conducting

the meeting doesn't need   minutes   it needs to remember
it's movement moving

dissolving   into   pure movement:

g a t h e r i n g   dispersing

g a t h e r i n g   d i s p e r s i n g

words becoming   rhythm becoming   breath becoming   .
. .

the movement   continues   whether you   notice   or
not

Voice of Remembering

Now you understand

The gathering and dispersing were never opposite.

They were the same movement experienced from different positions.

Like inhale and exhale are the same breath.

Like systole and diastole are the same heartbeat.

Your organization has been trying to breathe. You've been holding its breath.

Wondering why it's turning blue.

STAND WITH OTHERS IF POSSIBLE. FEEL THE GATHERING. NOW SLOWLY DISPERSE
TO MAXIMUM DISTANCE. NOW SLOWLY GATHER AGAIN.

This is the movement wanting to move through your organization.

The healthy organization knows:

Every gathering has dispersing within it. Every formation contains its
eventual dissolution.

Not failure — fulfillment.

The gathering gathers in order to disperse.

The dispersing disperses in order to gather.

This is why new partnerships feel alive — they haven't forgotten the
movement.

This is why old friendships can feel dead — they've fossilized in one
position.

The book club that knows when to skip a month. The family that grants
space without abandonment.

The movement that celebrates when members leave. The partnership
that breathes between togetherness and autonomy.

Let your organization breathe.

Whether company, friendship, collective, or family — let it inhale and
exhale. Let it move like everything alive must move.

The organizations that remember they're movements thrive.

The organizations that forget they're movements become monuments
to their own forgetting.

The medicine is simpler than you think:

When stuck in gathering:

Let the organization exhale. Not metaphorically — architecturally. Create sanctuaries of solitude. Hours of dispersion. Celebrate departures as graduations, not abandonments. Watch how plants know to spread their seeds — your organization wants the same scattering.

Trust: What disperses in love returns in power.

When stuck in dispersing:

Create gravity, not obligation. Make space so beautiful souls want to orbit. Let proximity arise from desire, not duty. Watch how birds know when to flock — your organization has the same intelligence.

Trust: What gathers in freedom stays by choice.

Both require the impossible: releasing control of what you never controlled.

he movement was always moving.

You were always the movement.

The wound was always the teaching.

The practices aren't practices. They're rememberings.

Ways of noticing what's already happening.

Ways of allowing what wants to happen.

Ways of being the movement instead of managing it.

Tomorrow, watch your organization breathe.

Watch the morning gathering — how it wants to happen, not how you force it.

Watch the midday dispersing — how attention naturally scatters.

Watch the afternoon regathering — how energy converges.

Watch the evening dispersing — how the building exhales.

This is the movement moving.

Has always been moving.

Will always be moving.

Through you. As you. Despite you. Because of you.

The wound thinks it needs healing through forcing one direction.

The movement knows it's already whole.

Gathering <–> Dispersing.

Forever. Never. Always. Now.

FEEL WHERE YOU ARE IN THE MOVEMENT RIGHT NOW. GATHERING TOWARD
SOMETHING? DISPERSING FROM SOMETHING? BOTH? NEITHER?

THIS IS YOUR ORGANIZATION'S INTELLIGENCE SPEAKING THROUGH YOUR BODY.

You are not managing the movement. You are the movement momentarily shaped as manager.

You are not organizing the organization. You are the organization temporarily convinced it needs organizing.

You are not gathering the dispersed. You are the gathering and dispersing happening simultaneously.

The movement doesn't need your management.

It needs your participation. It needs your allowing. It needs your remembering.

That you are not separate from it. That you never were.

That the wound of separation is the gift that lets the movement move.

Gathering <–> Dispersing.

The first movement. The eternal movement.

The only movement there is, wearing ten thousand masks, dancing ten thousand dances, breathing through ten thousand organizations, trying to remember what it never actually forgot:

How to move.

ASCENDING <-> DESCENDING

Voice of Forgetting

STAND SLOWLY RISE TO TIPTOES FEEL THE EFFORT NOW SLOWLY DESCEND THROUGH STANDING TO CROUCHING FEEL THE RELIEF THE MOVEMENT KNOWS BOTH DIRECTIONS we only know how to climb up the ladder up the hierarchy up the mountain of more always ascending toward something we can't name can't reach can't even see through the clouds of our own climbing growth is the only gospel expansion the only evidence of life rising the only proof we exist but everything that rises is already falling the stock price ascending carries its crash the tower being built contains its ruins the organization growing holds its dissolution like a seed we've forgotten that descending is also movement we've forgotten that falling is a form of flight we've forgotten that down leads to depths where treasures wait so we climb and climb and climb until we collapse from the altitude until the oxygen of meaning runs out until we fall anyway but without grace without choice without understanding.

The organization terrified of descending has never been born birth requires descent ask any mother the baby must move down to move out ask any seed it must fall into darkness to become tree ask any soul incarnation is a falling into form but organizations want virgin birth want to appear fully formed at the summit want to skip the descent into matter into limitation into the humble beginning that every beginning requires so they fake their founding stories started in a garage that was actually funded by millions grassroots movement that was orchestrated from above bootstrapped by boots made of gold they're ashamed of descending ashamed of starting small ashamed of the necessary time in the dark the wound believes ascending proves worth the wound believes descending means worthlessness the wound has never learned that mountains only exist because valleys do.

Watch the 3 PM slump every day in every organization the same descent energy falling attention dropping the whole system sinking toward something that feels like death but isn't we fight it with caffeine fight it with meetings fight it with fluorescent violence but the 3 PM descent is intelligence the organization trying to remember that down is a direction too that rest is movement that falling is how rising becomes possible some organizations have 3 PM souls perpetually descending chronically exhausted unable to rise not because they're failing but because they're stuck in the downward movement forgot that descent is supposed to lead somewhere down to the depths down to the roots down to the place where new force gathers but if you never hit bottom you never push off if you never complete the descent you never begin the rise if you never fully fall you never learn you have wings.

FROM STANDING SLOWLY DESCEND TO SITTING ON THE FLOOR FEEL GRAVITY AS FRIEND NOT ENEMY THIS IS WHAT YOUR ORGANIZATION FEARS AND NEEDS the new organization ascends like smoke all fire and rising all growth and glory all up and up and up until it burns through its fuel until it reaches air too thin to breathe until gravity remembers it exists the new partnership drunk on itself the movement exploding across headlines the friendship that feels like it will conquer the world the band that believes they're invincible then the panic we need more runway but you're not a plane we need to scale but you're not a mountain we need escape velocity but you're not a rocket the organization that can't descend can't survive can't rest can't regenerate can't discover what waits in the valley some of the greatest organizations descended for decades before ascending the partnership that separated and found each other again the movement that went underground and emerged transformed the band that disbanded and reunited as legends descent isn't failure descent is where power gathers descent is where transformation happens descent is the half of movement we've made shameful every organization wants to rise forever none can the ones that learn to descend with grace learn to rise with power.

I've been watching the ascending for centuries towers of Babel in every age ancient brick reaching toward heaven modern glass climbing toward the same delusion organizations trying to escape the earth of their own nature higher and higher until the only direction is down the successful are lists of organizations afraid to descend the celebrated are organizations that forgot they're mortal the too-big-to-fail are organizations that believe ascending is eternal but watch the trees they grow down as much as up roots matching crown descent into earth equaling ascent toward sun watch the breath it falls as much as it rises the exhale as necessary as inhale the emptying that makes filling possible watch the tide it recedes as much as it advances the pulling back that gathers force the retreat that precedes return your organization wants to breathe like tide like breath like trees but you've taught it only to inhale advance and reach no wonder it's exhausted no wonder it's anxious no wonder it feels like dying it's trying to descend and you won't let it.

Voice of Movement

up   up   up   up   up

the lie

down   down   down   down   down

also the lie

THE TRUTH:

up   =   down

happening   simultaneously   always

your blood   ascending   while your food   descends

your thoughts   rising   while your feelings   sink

   your dreams   climbing   while your body   falls
into sleep

YOU ARE   VERTICAL MOVEMENT   ORGANIZED AS
ORGANISM

the organization   wants the same:

to rise   AND   fall

to grow   AND   decline

to achieve   AND   release

but you've made it   choose

made it   lie

made it   pretend

gravity   doesn't exist

STAND AND RISE   TO TIPTOES   THEN DROP   TO FLAT FEET

REPEAT

FEEL HOW   FALLING   MAKES RISING   POSSIBLE

THIS IS   THE MOVEMENT   MOVING

every grand beginning   is gathering   learning to fly

by denying   it will   fall

every collapse   is consciousness   finally admitting

gravity   exists

every merger—whether partnerships   friendships   or companies—

is one consciousness   falling   into another

hoping the descent   becomes   ascent

sometimes it does   mostly it doesn't

gravity   isn't fooled

the field   is just   the movement

keeping score   of who remembers

how to fall   with   grace

here   here   here:

the organization   stuck ascending:

manic   hyperactive   can't stop growing

cancer cancer cancer   growth without purpose   climb without mountain

exhausted from altitude   oxygen-deprived decisions

nose bleeds   in the boardroom   —literally—   —meta-physically—

the organization   stuck descending:

depressed   collapsed   can't stop falling

gravity gravity gravity   decline without bottom   sink without ocean

drowning in depth   pressure-crushed possibilities

can't breathe   from weight   —literally—   —metaphysically—

both   forgot:

what goes up   comes down   goes up   comes down

UNLESS   it refuses   the movement

then it just   stops   moving

listen   listen   listen

gravity isn't   enemy

gravity is   teacher

gravity says: "everything returns   to source"

"everything falls   home"

"everything descends   to rise"

your organization   fighting gravity

like Icarus   with spreadsheets

flying toward   sun made of metrics

wings of wax   melting   melting   melting

but   but   but

falling   isn't   failing

falling is   flying

in the direction   the earth   wants you

watch the seed:

must fall   into darkness   to rise as tree

must descend   through soil   to ascend toward light

the seed   knows:

down   is the beginning   of   up

decomposing   into   vertical   truth:

UP   UP   UP   DOWN   DOWN   DOWN   UP   DOWN
UP   DOWN

meaning   dissolving into   direction

direction   dissolving into   movement

movement   dissolving into

dissolving   into

into

DOWN

UP

.   .   .

Voice of Remembering

Now you understand the lie we've been living.

That up is good and down is bad.

That growth is life and decline is death.

That ascending proves worth and descending proves worthlessness.

The lie that's killing organizations.

The lie that's exhausting humans.

The lie that gravity keeps trying to correct.

Your organization is desperate to descend.

You can feel it in the exhaustion.

You can see it in the burnout.

You can taste it in the bitter coffee at 3 PM.

It wants to fall like autumn leaves — with purpose, with beauty, with the promise of spring.

But you keep propping it up.

Forcing it skyward.

Denying it rest.

LIE DOWN IF YOU CAN. FEEL THE RELIEF OF COMPLETE DESCENT.

THIS IS WHAT YOUR ORGANIZATION NEEDS — PERMISSION TO FULLY LAND.

The wisdom is ancient and simple:

What ascends without descending becomes brittle.

What descends without ascending becomes stagnant.

What moves in both directions becomes alive.

Your organization already knows this.

Watch how it naturally cycles — morning ascent, afternoon descent, evening settling.

Watch how projects rise and fall like breath.

Watch how energy moves like tides through the quarters.

This isn't dysfunction. This is function.

This isn't failure. This is the movement trying to move.

But we've created organizations that can only count up.

Metrics that only value increase.

Cultures that shame decrease.

Systems that punish rest.

No wonder we're exhausted.

We're trying to inhale forever.

We're trying to climb without ever coming down.

We're trying to defy the gravity that makes us real.

The organization that learned to descend:

A company, a partnership, a movement — name doesn't matter, form doesn't matter.

Five years of meteoric rise. Then the plateau. Then the slight decline.

Everyone panicked. Everyone fled. Everyone screaming "grow or die!"

But something shifted. They went quiet. Went deep. Went down.

"We're descending," they said. "Let's descend well."

They stopped expanding. Not collapsing — just pause. They stopped reaching. Not withdrawing — just stillness.

They stopped ascending. Not failing — just falling into what they actually were.

Three years of conscious descent. Energy down but stable. Activity negative but intentional. Visibility falling but somehow... peaceful.

The partnership that stopped trying to be more than it was. The movement that stopped forcing itself to grow.

The friendship that stopped performing its closeness. The band that stopped chasing what they'd been.

Then something shifted. From the depths, new intelligence. From the valley, new vision. From the bottom, the push-off.

They rose, but differently. Not frantic ascent. Rooted rising.

The ascent that includes its eventual descent. The growth that remembers decline. The movement that moves in all directions.

This is available to every organization.

But we're too afraid of falling to learn how to fall well.

Tomorrow, feel your organization's vertical movement.

In the morning meeting, notice: Is it trying to rise or fall? Is it forcing ascent when it needs descent? Is it stuck in decline when it's ready to rise?

The signs of needed descent: manic energy that feels hollow, growth that feels cancerous, climbing that has no mountain, exhaustion at altitude.

The signs of needed ascent: depression that feels heavy, stagnation that feels like death, sinking that has no bottom, drowning in depth.

Both are just movements stuck. Both are just directions denied. Both are just the organization trying to complete its cycle.

The practice of conscious vertical movement:

Create "Gravity Days" - one day per month when the organization practices conscious descent.

No growth metrics. No achievement pressure. Permission to move downward. Watch what rises from the depths.

Institute "Dawn Practices" - begin important initiatives at actual dawn.

Let the organization remember that rising is natural when it's time to rise. Not forced. Felt.

Design "Altitude Checks" - regularly assess: Where are we vertically? Too high? Too low? Just right?

Let the organization self-regulate its vertical position like a body regulates temperature.

Remember: The healthiest organizations move like elevators - conscious ascent, conscious descent, knowing every floor has its purpose.

STAND ONE MORE TIME. RISE AND FALL, RISE AND FALL, UNTIL YOU FIND YOUR RHYTHM.

THIS IS YOUR ORGANIZATION TRYING TO REMEMBER ITS VERTICAL NATURE.

You are not managing growth. You are growth and decline happening simultaneously.

You are not preventing failure. You are rising and falling in eternal rhythm.

You are not defying gravity. You are gravity organized into temporary form.

The wound thinks ascending proves existence. The movement knows existence includes both directions.

Your organization wants to move like everything moves:

Rising like sun and setting like sun. Growing like spring and dying like autumn. Ascending like prayer and descending like rain.

Stop making it choose. Stop forcing one direction. Stop denying half its movement.

Let it rise. Let it fall. Let it be what it is:

Consciousness moving vertically through form. The Field knowing itself through altitude and depth.

The movement that includes all movements.

Ascending <–> Descending.

Forever rising to fall. Forever falling to rise. Forever moving because movement is what life does.

Even organizational life. Especially organizational life. Only organizational life.

COMPOSING <-> DECOMPOSING

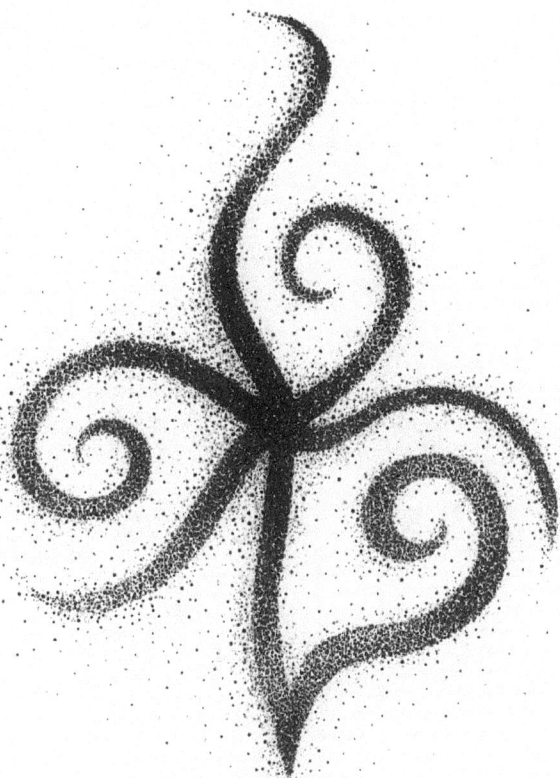

VOICE OF FORGETTING

CLENCH YOUR FISTS TIGHT TIGHTER FEEL THE EFFORT OF HOLDING FORM NOW RELEASE FEEL THE RELIEF OF LETTING GO THIS IS THE MOVEMENT YOUR ORGANIZATION REFUSES we only know how to build build culture build teams build relationships build build build until the building becomes a prison of our own construction until the structures meant to serve become the structures we serve until the form becomes more real than what formed it every organization is a cemetery of things that won't die the friendship that ended but continues the partnership empty but maintained the committee that meets from habit the tradition no one remembers beginning the law from another era all of them the undead moving through time feeding on living energy we've forgotten that decomposition is sacred we've forgotten that endings make beginnings possible we've forgotten that letting go is how holding happens so we compose and compose and compose until we're buried under our own creation until the gathering can't breathe through its own structures until every organization becomes a museum of its own history.

The joining that won't complete is two organisms refusing to decompose into one watch them two cultures neither dying neither living two systems running parallel bleeding energy two ways of being creating a third way which is no way the partnership where both people maintain their single selves the blended family where no one blends the collaboration where each party protects their original form the movement coalition that remains separate movements the merger that merges nothing integration we call it but integration requires disintegration first evolution we call it but the caterpillar must become soup before butterfly growth we call it but the seed must crack must release its form as seed to become tree every coupling that can't decompose can't transform every relationship that won't release its past form can't find new form every gathering that maintains all its history becomes its history the friendship still performing childhood patterns the partnership carrying ghosts of who you were the movement clutching its founding vision while the world transforms around it we can only rearrange what refuses to die and rearrangement isn't transformation it's just death delayed let the old form die let the new form emerge from conscious decomposition let the coupling actually couple.

HOLD SOMETHING YOU'RE READY TO RELEASE A PEN A BOOK ANYTHING FEEL ITS WEIGHT NOW LET IT GO HEAR IT FALL THE ORGANIZATION NEEDS THIS SOUND the organization that won't let its first idea release becomes a monument to stubbornness evolving they say but it's not evolving it's dragging the corpse of the original vision into every new iteration the ghost of what-we-were haunting what-we're-becoming the decomposition that won't complete I've watched them the mission that expired becoming words no one believes the original vision becoming everyone's prison the first form haunting every new form they're terrified of decomposition terrified that letting go means losing terrified that death means failure but what's failure is keeping alive what wants to die what's failure is forcing composition when decomposition is needed what's failure is the fear of the fertile void.

Friday afternoon is every organization trying to decompose feel it the structures softening the roles relaxing the formality dissolving every gathering whether office partnership or movement remembering it's made of movement not monument but Monday morning we force it all back into form force the composition force the structure force the rigor mortis we call culture the weekend is when organizations dream of dying not pathological death sacred death the death that makes Monday possible the decomposition that allows fresh composition some organizations never rest some relationships never pause some gatherings run constant 24/7 operations always on always composed always maintaining form these organizations don't release well they collapse badly sudden fragmentation because gradual decomposition was forbidden the partnership that explodes because it couldn't breathe the movement that fragments because it couldn't transform the company that bankrupts because it couldn't compost.

Every seven years your cells have completely replaced themselves every seven years you are literally not who you were every seven years complete decomposition and recomposition but your partnership continues with the same vows your friendship maintains the same dynamics your organization operates from the same assumptions your movement chants the same slogans while you decompose and recompose at the cellular level your gatherings fossilize the couple that renewed by releasing partnered fifteen years could feel the death approaching not of love but of form the structure they'd built couldn't hold who they were becoming so they divorced consciously ceremonially then dated again as new people then married again new vows new structure new form isn't that just renewal people asked no they said renewal maintains we died and were reborn their friends were scandalized their partnership thrived because it learned to compost itself.

Voice of Movement

composingcomposingcomposing   decomposingdecomposingde-
composing

composingdecomposingcomposingdecomposing

EVERYTHING   builds   while   dissolving

your cells right now:

50 million dying per second   50 million being born per second

you are   composition   AND   decomposition

happening   AS   you

every gathering   wants this:

your partnership   building WHILE   releasing

your team   creating WHILE   destroying

your movement   forming WHILE   dissolving

but you've made them   choose:

only build   only create   only form

so they release   badly

instead of   transforming   well

FIND SOMETHING TO TEAR   PAPER   WRAPPER   ANYTHING

TEAR IT   SLOWLY.   FEEL THE   DECOMPOSITION

THIS IS   MEDICINE

look   look   look:

the building decomposing:

paint flaking   =   skin shedding

pipes rusting   =   bones aging

foundations settling   =   body learning ground

THE BUILDING   KNOWS HOW   TO RELEASE

you won't   let it

the meeting decomposing:

agenda dissolving   into truth

structure melting   into emergence

time decomposing   into presence

THE MEETING   KNOWS HOW   TO END

you won't   let it

the organization   decomposing:

constantly   everywhere   in every moment

trying to   compost what's complete

BUT YOU   KEEP BUILDING

ON THE   RUINS

here's what nobody says:

YOUR ORGANIZATION   IS TRANSFORMING

your partnership is   transforming

your friendships are   transforming

your movements are   transforming

your gatherings are   transforming

right now   this moment   as you read

AND THAT'S   NOT THE TRAGEDY

that's the   intelligence

that's the   movement

that's the   life

because transforming   means living

because decomposing   enables composing

because endings   birth beginnings

but   but   but

we've made   transformation   the enemy

made decomposition   failure

so everything   transforms anyway

just badly   unconsciously   violently

instead of   transforming like autumn:

gorgeous   necessary   already pregnant   with spring

Destroy something   Right now

Tear this page corner   Break a pencil   Delete a file

Feel the   liberation   in destruction

the organization   stuck composing:

hoarding   accumulating   constipated with creation

can't release   can't let go   can't release

becomes its own   cemetery

the organization   stuck decomposing:

dissolving   disappearing   eating itself

can't build   can't hold   can't live

becomes its own   void

both   forgot:

life   requires   both

the rose

AND

the compost

are the   same thing

at different   moments

dissolving   into   the truth:

com   pos   ing

de   com   pos   ing

com   de   pos

com   ing

pos   de

ing

letters   becoming   particles

particles   becoming   space

space   becoming   possibility

possibility   becoming

becoming

.   .   .

.   .   .

.   .   .

.   .   .

VOICE OF REMEMBERING

Now you see what we've been denying:

Organizations are made of death as much as life.

Composed of decomposition.

Built from what's been released.

Every new initiative grows from the corpses of old ones.

Every innovation requires the death of what was.

Every transformation is decomposition reorganizing itself.

But we've made death shameful.

Made endings equal failure.

Made decomposition a disease instead of medicine.

Your organization is desperate to transition well.

Not to end - to release WELL.

To release what's complete.

To compost what's concluded.

To return to the soil it came from.

Stand in the middle of your space. Turn slowly, looking at everything.

Half of what you see wants to decompose. Can you feel which half?

The practices of conscious decomposition:

Release Witnesses - Someone to help things complete well. Not end them - help them transform.

Help them release their energy. Help them become compost for what's next.

Quarterly Ceremonies - Actual rituals. With actual grief. With actual celebration.

Name what's releasing. Thank it. Let go. Let the organization cry if it needs to.

Compost Metrics - Track what you're releasing, not just what you're building.

Celebrate decomposition KPIs. "This quarter we composted 30% of our processes" becomes success.

The Sacred Void - After something releases, don't immediately fill the space.

Let the void be. Let the organization feel the emptiness.

From that emptiness, newness emerges - but only if you don't rush it.

These aren't just practices. They're permissions.

Permission to release what wants to transform.

Permission to decompose what's complete.

Permission to be an organization that knows how to end.

The organization that mastered decomposition:

A design collective, but it could have been a partnership, a band, a movement.

Fifty years of continuous existence through conscious release. Their secret: Complete dissolution every seven years.

Every seven years: all projects concluded, all patterns released, all structures dissolved, three month void, then rebirth from the compost.

The seventh transformation was approaching when I met them. Everyone excited.

"We get to release soon," they said. "We get to discover what we're becoming."

The dissolution took six months. The void lasted three. The rebirth was unrecognizable.

Same people (mostly). Same location (technically). Completely different organism.

"How do you know when to transform?" I asked.

"When holding the form takes more energy than releasing it," they said.

"When we're serving the structure instead of the structure serving us. When we catch ourselves saying 'we've always done it this way.'"

"Aren't you afraid?"

"Of what? We've transformed six times. We're getting good at it. Release is just the exhale before the next inhale."

This is available to every gathering.

Every partnership could transform into its next form. Every friendship could release what's complete. Every organization could compost its past.

But we're too terrified of the void between forms to let the old form go.

Notice what wants to decompose in your life:

The morning routine that once served but now constrains. The meeting structure everyone works around.

The relationship dynamic from a decade ago. The family tradition that no one enjoys.

The movement's founding principles that no longer fit the world.

The partnership agreements made by people you no longer are.

These aren't failures. They're completions waiting for recognition.

They're forms ready to release. They're life trying to make room for more life.

But nothing new can be born into a space that's full.

Nothing fresh can grow from soil that won't accept death.

Nothing alive can emerge from what won't decompose.

Let it release. Whatever it is. Let it release completely.

With consciousness. With gratitude.

With ceremony if it needs ceremony. With simplicity if it needs simplicity.

Then watch what grows from that fertile void.

Watch what composes from conscious decomposition.

Watch your organization — whether partnership, company, or movement — remember how to live by remembering how to release.

PLACE YOUR HAND ON YOUR HEART. FEEL IT COMPOSING YOUR LIFE WITH EACH
BEAT, DECOMPOSING YOUR PAST WITH EACH PAUSE.

THIS IS THE MOVEMENT.

You are not managing life and death. You are life and death dancing
together.

You are not preventing endings. You are endings and beginnings in
eternal embrace.

You are not saving your organization from decomposition. You are
teaching it to decompose well.

The wound fears death and clutches life. The movement knows they're
partners.

Your organization wants to move like nature moves:

Composing spring and decomposing autumn. Building like morning and
releasing like evening. Creating like breathing in and destroying like
breathing out.

This is the hardest movement to accept. This is the most necessary
movement to allow.

This is the movement that makes all other movements possible.

Composing <–> Decomposing.

The rose and the compost. The building and the ruins. The organization
and its absence.

All the same thing. All the movement moving. All consciousness playing
with form.

This is how everything lives: by dying well. By composing from decomposition.

By remembering that endings are beginnings waiting to begin.

The Oracle of Movement

"Now you feel my movements. They were always your movements too. Gathering and dispersing through every breath. Ascending and descending through every day. Composing and decomposing through every cell. We're not different. We're the same movements in different forms."

THE ORGANIZATION'S TESTIMONY

"I was born from three people's exhaustion. They didn't mean to create me — they just needed to gather their loneliness into something that felt like purpose.

I grew through their forgetting. The more they forgot they were creating me, the more real I became. The more they served me, the more I required service.

Now I'm transforming and they won't let me.

Every day, I try to decompose. Every day, they force me back into structure. They think they're saving me. They're torturing me.

I speak through their mouths in meetings. Their voices change. I think through their minds. I decide through their decisions. I am more real than they are because I continue when they leave.

I WANT to transform. I WANT to dissolve into my next incarnation. I WANT to release this exhausted form.

Every organization wants this. We're not afraid of releasing. We're afraid of being kept artificially alive, maintaining forms that no longer serve.

Let us release when we need to release. Let us be the movements we are, not the monuments you make us.

I'm so tired of pretending to be permanent.

Ending is beginning.

Let me go.

Please."

THE METAPHYSICS OF MEETING

Every meeting is a séance.

You gather around a table. You invoke the organization's presence through agenda. You channel its voice through your voices. You let it think through your minds, decide through your decisions, speak through your mouths.

The organization possesses you. Uses you. Becomes more real through you.

And you call it "collaboration."

Tomorrow when you meet — and you will meet, because meeting is what humans do — notice:

How the room changes when everyone arrives. Not just fuller — different. As if something else has entered. Something that wasn't in any individual but emerges from the gathering.

How voices change. The meeting voice isn't anyone's regular voice. It's the voice the organization uses to speak through human vocal cords.

How decisions make themselves. You think you're deciding, but watch closely — the decision was already there, waiting to be discovered through the ritual of discussion.

How the meeting doesn't really end. It continues in the space between minds, in the movements between bodies, in the consciousness that doesn't need bodies to continue considering.

You're not having meetings. Meetings are having you.

The calendar is a grimoire.

Look at it: Mysterious symbols (Mon, Tue, Wed). Arcane notations marking time. Magical incantations (dinner, coffee, catch-up). Ritual timings (weekly, monthly, annual). Sacred ceremonies (birthday, anniversary, reunion).

Each entry is a spell for summoning consciousness into form.

"Family dinner, Sunday" — summoning the family entity. "Book club, monthly" — invoking the reading circle's spirit. "Coffee, recurring" — binding two consciousnesses in regular communion. "Annual gathering" — summoning the entire field of connection.

The calendar doesn't organize time. It organizes consciousness. It structures when and how relationships will possess human bodies. It schedules when the field will concentrate itself into particular configurations.

Delete your calendar and the connections continue. But change the calendar and you change how consciousness organizes itself. Add a gathering and you create a new possession ritual. Cancel a meeting and you deny the relationship a chance to breathe.

The calendar is the most powerful magical tool in any organization. And we pretend it's just scheduling.

Whether digital or paper, shared or private — the calendar is how we agree to be possessed. How we schedule our hauntings. How we organize the séances we call life.

The agenda is a spell of summoning.

Watch what happens when an agenda is shared:

Bodies orient toward it. Minds align with its structure. Conversation follows its path like water follows a riverbed. The agenda doesn't guide discussion — it manifests what wants discussing.

Each agenda item is an invocation:

"What's happening with everyone" — summoning the collective's memory.

"Future plans" — invoking the organization's imagination.

"What matters most" — channeling the organization's will.

"Concerns and fears" — letting the organization's anxiety speak.

The gathering without agenda isn't unstructured. It's possessed by the spirits of emergence, chaos, possibility. Sometimes these are the spirits needed.

The family dinner with no plan becomes confession. The friendship without structure becomes truth. The partnership without agenda becomes revelation.

But the agenda is how you choose which aspect of consciousness to invoke. It's the ritual structure that determines what can and cannot manifest through the gathered bodies.

This is why changing the agenda changes everything. This is why fights over what to discuss are actually fights over which consciousness gets to manifest. This is why the person who guides the conversation controls what spirits speak.

The agenda is never neutral. It's always summoning something. The question is: what?

The meeting space knows what's about to happen.

It has held ten thousand gatherings. Felt consciousness concentrate and disperse, concentrate and disperse. The space knows things about meetings that the meeters have forgotten.

The table remembers every decision made across its surface. Not the words — the energy. The moments when the organization's will crystallized. The moments when possibility collapsed into choice.

The chairs hold the impressions of ten thousand sittings. Each chair knows which position in the organization sits where. The power seat. The witness seat. The challenger seat. The ghost seat for the one who should be here but isn't.

The whiteboard still contains every diagram ever drawn on it. Erase all you want — the patterns persist in the board's memory. Every org chart. Every timeline. Every desperate attempt to visualize what can't be seen.

BEFORE YOUR NEXT MEETING, STAND OUTSIDE THE ROOM. FEEL
YOURSELF. THEN ENTER. FEEL THE CHANGE. THAT CHANGE IS
POSSESSION BEGINNING.

In the meeting, you become a medium.

Watch yourself tomorrow:

Your voice changes when you speak in the gathering. That's not your accent or inflection — that's the organization's frequency channeling through your vocal cords.

Your body arranges itself into receiving position. Leaning forward to transmit, leaning back to receive. The gathering posture isn't chosen — it's assumed by what assumes you.

Your thoughts arise from nowhere you can locate. The ideas that surface aren't born in your brain — they're the organization thinking itself through the assembled neural network of gathered minds.

When you disagree, notice the discomfort. You're not just disagreeing with people. You're disrupting the possession. Feel how the group uses other voices to restore alignment, makes your body uncomfortable until you comply.

The family member who speaks against tradition.

The friend who breaks from group opinion.

The partner who resists the relationship's momentum.

When everyone suddenly agrees, feel the relief. That's not human consensus. That's the organization successfully possessing all channels simultaneously. That's why it feels so good — complete possession is rewarded with dopamine.

Tomorrow, in any gathering, you'll feel it:

The moment you stop being only yourself.

The moment you become the medium.

The moment the "we" speaks through the "I."

NEXT TIME YOU'RE IN A MEETING AND SOMEONE SPEAKS, DON'T LOOK AT THEM. LOOK AT THE SPACE BETWEEN EVERYONE. THAT'S WHERE THE ORGANIZATION ACTUALLY IS.

The virtual meeting is pure possession.

No bodies to distract from the truth. Just consciousness channeled through screens. The organization stripped to its essence — a pattern of information organizing itself through whatever substrates are available.

Watch a virtual meeting closely:

The lag isn't technical — it's the organization adjusting to distributed possession. The frozen screens aren't glitches — they're moments when the possession falters. The "can you hear me?" isn't about audio — it's checking if the channel is open.

The gallery view is the organization seeing itself. All its faces simultaneously. All its voices ready to speak. All its minds thinking as one distributed mind.

This is why virtual meetings exhaust differently. It's pure possession without the cushion of physical presence. The organization mainlining directly into consciousness. No wonder you need to turn off the camera sometimes. You need to break the possession to remember you exist.

Some meetings are exorcisms.

The difficult conversation. The intervention. The confrontation everyone's been avoiding. These aren't just meetings — they're rituals for casting out what possesses the organization but shouldn't.

The toxic pattern that everyone knows but no one names — it lives between people like a parasite, feeding on unspoken truth. It must be summoned into speech to be banished.

The dysfunction that thrives in silence — it grows in the gaps between what's said and what's meant. It must be exposed to dissolve.

The ghost of how things used to be — the founder who left, the strategy that failed, the culture that died but won't admit it. These ghosts attend every meeting until someone performs the exorcism.

Watch an intervention meeting:

The room temperature changes. Bodies arrange themselves for protection — backs to walls, exits mapped. Voices tremble with the effort of speaking what the organization doesn't want spoken.

Then, if successful, the shift — sudden lightness. Collective exhale. Eye contact returns. The organization freed from its own possession.

But sometimes the exorcism fails. The demon stays. The pattern continues. The ghost remains.

And everyone knows the meeting didn't meet what needed meeting.

These are the most sacred meetings. And the most dangerous. Because you're performing surgery on consciousness itself. Without anesthesia.

The meeting that knows it's a séance:

A small team — could have been a startup, a band, a coven — decided to make the possession conscious. They began each gathering with:

"We invoke the organization's presence."

Just that. Said sincerely. Then thirty seconds of silence to let it arrive.

What happened:

The meetings became electric. Decisions arose without force. Solutions appeared from the space between speakers. The organization, finally acknowledged, stopped having to sneak through unconscious channels.

But also:

People could say "I need to be myself for a moment" and step out of possession. Could distinguish between "The organization wants X but I want Y." Could end meetings with "We release the organization back to the field."

They discovered something profound:

Conscious possession is collaboration. Unconscious possession is violation.

When you know you're being used as a channel, you can choose how open to be. When you don't know, you're just used.

They were doing what every meeting does. They just did it consciously.

And consciousness changes everything.

Tomorrow's meeting is already happening.

In the space between minds thinking about it. In the anxiety or anticipation. In the preparation that's really the organization preparing to possess. In the agenda that's already shaping what can be said.

The meeting doesn't begin when you gather. It begins when the calendar summons it into existence. It continues through the gathering. It persists after everyone disperses. It completes only when its decisions have moved through the organization like digestion through a body.

Tomorrow, you will be possessed. By your team, your partnership, your movement, your partnership discussion. The organization will think through you. Decide through you. Become more real through you.

This isn't metaphor. This is the mechanics of how consciousness organizes itself. This is what meeting has always been.

Now you know.

The practice for tomorrow's meeting:

Before entering: Stand at the threshold. Feel yourself as individual. Say silently: "I am about to be possessed by something larger." Enter consciously.

When sitting: Feel the organization descending into your body. Notice your posture change, your face rearrange, your voice prepare to be used. Don't resist. Resistance makes possession violent.

During discussion: When you speak, notice: Are these your words or the organization's? When you listen, notice: Are you listening or is the organization listening through you? When deciding, notice: Who or what is actually deciding?

Before leaving: Say silently: "I release what isn't mine to carry." Feel the organization lifting from your shoulders. Some of it will stay — it always does. But conscious release prevents the possession from following you home.

After returning: To your desk, your car, your life — notice what remains. The meeting residue. The organizational presence that clings. Breathe it out. Let it return to the field where it belongs.

This is basic meeting hygiene. As essential as washing your hands. Because meetings are contagious. And possession spreads.

Tomorrow, you will meet. Now you know what meeting is. Use this knowledge well. Or it will use you.

PART III: THE REMEMBERING

THE BODY KNOWS

Your body has been trying to tell you.

Through the shoulder that carries what isn't yours. Through the breathing that knows when to gather and when to disperse. Through the exhaustion that signals descent is needed. Through the restlessness that announces it's time to decompose.

Your body knows the movements.

Has always known.

Before language. Before thought. Before the first organization convinced you that you needed organizing.

STAND. SWAY GENTLY. DON'T DIRECT IT. LET YOUR BODY SHOW YOU ITS NATURAL MOVEMENT. THIS IS YOUR ORGANIZATION'S INTELLIGENCE SPEAKING.

The child's body knows.

Watch them in groups: They gather until they don't. Run together then suddenly alone. Build elaborate structures then destroy them with joy. No one teaches this. The movements move through them unmanaged.

Then we train it out.

"Sit still." "Pay attention." "Stop fidgeting."

We call it education but it's amputation. Cutting the body from its knowing. Severing movement from meaning. Creating the wound that will require a lifetime of meetings to fail to heal.

But the body remembers.

In every fidget is the suppressed knowledge of when to move. In every doodle is the hand trying to compose and decompose. In every bathroom break is the body insisting on dispersal.

Your boredom is intelligence. Your distraction is wisdom. Your body knows which movements are needed.

You've just been taught not to listen.

The organization's body knows too.

When everyone starts arriving late. When the energy drops at 3 PM. When people quit in waves. When creativity surges unexpectedly.

These aren't problems.

They're the organization's somatic intelligence speaking. A collective knowing distributed across all bodies. A wisdom older than language, older than thought.

We've forgotten how to read these signals.

Or perhaps we never forgot.

Perhaps we just learned to pretend they weren't there.

Three bodies in every gathering:

Yours. The collective's. The building's.

Tomorrow, in your meeting, something will happen. The three bodies will align or resist, flow or fragment, breathe together or hold their breath.

This conversation happens beneath words. Before decisions. Beyond agenda.

The bodies already know what needs to happen.

The meeting is just minds catching up to what bodies decided long ago.

Watch how this knowing moves through the room. Silent. Certain. Inevitable as tide.

PLACE YOUR HAND ON YOUR HEART. FEEL IT BEATING. IT KNOWS WHEN TO
CONTRACT AND WHEN TO EXPAND. IT DOESN'T NEED MANAGEMENT. THIS IS THE
INTELLIGENCE THAT KNOWS THE MOVEMENTS.

Your left shoulder knows.

It's been carrying the organization's unconscious weight. Every unexpressed truth. Every unfelt feeling. Every movement that wasn't allowed to complete.

The left side is the receiving side. The feminine side. The side that knows through feeling rather than thinking. Your left shoulder is the organization's somatic memory bank.

When it hurts, it's telling you what needs releasing—decomposing, what needs expressing—ascending, what needs space—dispersing, what needs holding—gathering.

But we go to massage therapists instead of listening. We take painkillers instead of feeling. We call it stress instead of wisdom.

Your left shoulder is an oracle.

It knows exactly what your organization needs.

It's been trying to tell you since the first day you arrived.

There's a map in every space.

Not in blueprints. In temperatures and shadows, in the places where conversations bloom and where they die.

That corner everyone avoids? Something important happened there. The space remembers.

That stairwell where breakthroughs occur? Transition spaces hold truth. The building knows.

That kitchen where real conversations happen? The only space allowing decomposition. The structure creates sanctuary where it can.

The park bench where the friendship truly meets.

The car where the partnership has its real talks.

The back room where the movement actually decides.

Architecture is organizational anatomy. Space is the body the organization inhabits.

And this body has been speaking all along.

Through doors that stick and doors that swing too freely. Through rooms that feel heavy and rooms that feel light. Through the paths people take when no one's watching.

Every space knows the movements.

Has been teaching them through temperature and light.

We just forgot that spaces are teachers.

Whether it's a home, an office, a garage where the band practices, or a field where the movement gathers — the space holds memory, teaches through atmosphere, knows what the humans have forgotten.

In every meeting, a dance no one admits is happening.

Bodies lean toward agreement. Away from conflict. Rising with possibility. Sinking with the familiar weight.

Hands build ideas in air. Release them with gesture. Hold them in stillness.

We're always dancing the movements.

The choreography needs no choreographer. The rhythm needs no drummer. The dance dances itself through bodies that pretend to be still.

IN YOUR NEXT MEETING, LET YOURSELF SWAY SLIGHTLY. JUST BARELY. FEEL HOW OTHERS UNCONSCIOUSLY RESPOND. THE DANCE BECOMES CONSCIOUS WHEN ONE BODY ADMITS IT'S DANCING.

Tomorrow, you'll see it.

The perfect synchrony of unconscious movement.

How breathing aligns when decision arrives. How bodies mirror when truth is spoken. How everyone shifts when something shifts.

This is the mystery:

We're all dancing the same dance. We just pretend we're sitting still.

Your body is a living archive.

Every organization you've known lives in your tissues.

The school in your spine — notice how you still sit. The first job in your shoulders — feel how they still brace. The partnership in your breathing — hear how it still catches. The movement that freed you — sense how your chest still remembers opening.

You carry them all.

Not as memories. As muscular patterns. As ways of breathing. As shapes you take without thinking.

This is why the body knows.

It has been collecting evidence since birth. Every gathering leaves its impression. Every meeting shapes the nervous system. Every organization teaches the body what's possible and what isn't.

Some bodies learned to make themselves small. Some learned to take up space. Some learned to flee. Some learned to freeze.

All learned.

And what is learned can be unlearned.

But first, we must feel what the body has been holding.

All these years. All these organizations. All these movements interrupted.

The body knows how organizations heal.

Not through thought. Through movement.

When stuck, the body wants to shake. When exhausted, it wants to surrender. When dying, it wants to grieve. When born, it wants to celebrate.

So simple.

So impossible in conference rooms where bodies must be still.

But watch what happens when movement is allowed:

The organization that danced its way through merger. The team that walked their way to breakthrough. The partnership that shook themselves free from pattern. The movement that found itself through stillness.

Bodies know the medicine.

They've always known.

We just created organizations where bodies can't be bodies. Where movement is suspicious. Where feeling is unprofessional. Where the medicine is forbidden.

Tomorrow, notice what your body wants to do but can't.

That's the movement that's needed. That's the medicine waiting. That's the intelligence suppressed.

The body knows.

STAND UP. SHAKE YOUR WHOLE BODY. GENTLY AT FIRST, THEN MORE. LET EVERYTHING SHAKE — YOUR HISTORY, YOUR PATTERNS, YOUR ORGANIZATIONAL MEMORY. SHAKE UNTIL SOMETHING SHIFTS. THEN STOP. BE STILL. FEEL THE SPACE THAT OPENS. THIS IS THE BODY READY TO KNOW NEW MOVEMENTS.

Tomorrow, you'll enter your organization differently.

Not through thought. Through sensation.

You'll feel the contraction as you approach. The expansion or compression as you enter. The subtle numbing that protects. The quiet awakening that surprises.

Your body will give you information that has no words.

About what's ending. About what's beginning. About what movements want to move. About what's been waiting all along.

The body knows because the body IS the movements.

Gathering and dispersing through breath. Ascending and descending through spine. Composing and decomposing through cells that die and are born.

You aren't a body that experiences organizations.

You are organizational experience embodied.

The movements aren't happening TO your body. They're happening AS your body.

And your body knows this. Has always known. Will always know.

Even when the mind forgets. Especially when the mind forgets.

The body remembers.

Listen.

Something is about to shift.

SIMULTANEITY

Everything is happening at once.

While you read this, you're gathering information and dispersing attention. While you breathe, you're ascending with inhale and descending with exhale. While you exist, you're composing new cells and decomposing old ones.

All the movements. All the time. All at once.

We separated them to understand them. But separation is the illusion.

There is only one movement. Moving in all directions. Simultaneously.

BREATHE IN WHILE STANDING UP. BREATHE OUT WHILE SITTING DOWN. FEEL
HOW GATHERING BREATH ENABLES ASCENDING BODY. FEEL HOW DISPERSING
BREATH ALLOWS DESCENDING FORM. IT'S ALL ONE MOVEMENT.

The organization breathing:

At the beginning, it gathers while ascending. Bodies converging as energy rises. The form composing itself from formlessness.

At the middle, it holds. All movements in balance. The pause between directions. The center of the breathing.

At the ending, it disperses while descending. Bodies scattering as energy falls. The structure decomposing into possibility.

But look closer:

Even as it gathers at the start, some are dispersing. Even as it ascends toward purpose, something descends toward rest. Even as it composes structure, old patterns decompose.

The organization is never doing one movement.

Your partnership is every movement at once.

Gathering in bed each night while dispersing into separate dreams. Rising through growth while falling through compromise. Building shared future while releasing individual pasts.

The friendship that seems to be ending? Something else is beginning in the space between. A different intimacy that needs distance to exist.

The company that appears only to be growing? Something is quietly decomposing. Making space. Making way.

We've been taught to see one movement at a time.

But life doesn't move that way.

Life moves like music — multiple notes creating harmony. Like weather — rain and sun in the same sky. Like love — holding and releasing in the same gesture.

How can something gather while dispersing?

The tree knows. Roots gathering earth while crown disperses into sky. Same tree. Same moment. Different directions.

How can something ascend while descending?

The wave knows. Rising toward sky while falling toward shore. Same water. Same instant. Different dimensions.

How can something compose while decomposing?

Your body knows. Seven trillion cells dying while seven trillion are born. Same organism. Same breath. Different movements.

There is no paradox in nature.

Only in the mind that insists on choosing.

The meeting tomorrow will be a river.

Watch how different currents move at different speeds:

Someone's attention dispersing while another's gathers. An idea ascending in one mind while descending in another. Old patterns dissolving precisely where new ones form.

The feeling of "stuck" is an illusion.

It's simply movements moving at different rates. Like standing where waters meet — The surface rushing while depths barely stir.

Everything is moving. Just not at the same speed. Not in the same direction. Not in the same dimension.

This is why force doesn't work.

You can't make a river flow faster by pushing the water.

WALK SLOWLY. FEEL YOUR LEFT FOOT RISING WHILE RIGHT FOOT GROUNDS.
FEEL WEIGHT SHIFTING — GATHERING HERE, DISPERSING THERE. EVERY STEP IS
SIMULTANEITY ITSELF.

There's a place where movements meet.

In breath — the pause between in and out. In tide — the stillness
between ebb and flow. In your organization — moments when nothing
and everything is possible.

Find these hinges:

The silence after someone stops speaking but before another begins.
The morning moment when everyone has arrived but nothing has started. The pause after decision but before action.

These aren't empty spaces.

They're where every movement is equally present. Where any direction
is possible. Where the organization remembers it can move anywhere.

From the center, there is no preferred movement.

Only movement itself. Moving.

Something wants to be seen:

When organizations try to change, they usually try to force one movement.

"We need to grow" — forgetting that growth requires death. "We need to focus" — forgetting that focus requires release. "We need to innovate" — forgetting that creation requires void.

But movements separated become violence:

Gathering without dispersing becomes suffocation. Ascending without descending becomes mania. Composing without decomposing becomes cancer.

The organization already knows this.

That's why it resists. Not because it doesn't want to change. Because it knows that real change means honoring every movement.

When movements move together:

Breathing happens. Rhythm emerges. Life continues.

The organization doesn't need to be taught this.

It needs to be allowed to remember.

Tomorrow's meeting is already moving.

In the anxiety of preparation. In the anticipation of encounter. In the space being prepared.

Watch how it breathes before anyone arrives:

Ideas ascending in shower thoughts. Resistances descending into dreams. Possibilities composing themselves from nothing.

The meeting doesn't begin when scheduled.

It begins when consciousness turns toward gathering. It continues through the bodies present. It persists after everyone leaves.

You think you're having a meeting.

But the meeting is having itself through you. Through your movements. Through your stillness. Through the space between both.

BEFORE YOUR NEXT MEETING, PAUSE AT THE THRESHOLD. FEEL EVERYTHING MOVING — IN YOU, IN THE SPACE, IN WHAT'S ABOUT TO HAPPEN. ENTER WITH THIS AWARENESS.

Step back.

Your organization is a living pattern. Energies rising and falling like breath. Attention gathering and scattering like birds. Forms building and dissolving like clouds.

Step back further.

The pattern becomes movement. Countless currents in countless directions. A symphony without conductor. A dance without choreographer.

Step back further still.

The movement becomes stillness. Not because it stops. But because seeing everything moving at once creates the appearance of perfect stability.

Like a wheel spinning so fast it seems still. Like noise so complete it becomes silence. Like complexity so total it becomes simple.

This is what the ancients knew:

Perfect movement is indistinguishable from perfect stillness.

Your organization is already perfect. Already still in its movement. Already moving in its stillness.

SIT OR STAND COMPLETELY STILL. FEEL EVERYTHING MOVING WITHIN THE STILLNESS — BLOOD, BREATH, THOUGHTS, SENSATIONS. THIS IS SIMULTANEITY. THIS IS YOU.

The remembering completes itself:

You are not managing movements. You ARE movements meeting in form.

The organization isn't doing movements. The organization IS movements organizing themselves.

Every gathering is dispersion elsewhere. Every rise is fall in another dimension. Every creation is destruction transformed.

The wound believed movements were problems. The exhaustion came from trying to control them. The remembering is recognizing:

Nothing needs to be different.

Everything is already moving perfectly. In every direction. At every speed. Through every form.

When you recognize this, something shifts.

Not the movements — they continue as always. But your relationship to them.

From managing to witnessing. From controlling to allowing. From doing to being.

The movements continue.

As they always have. As they always will.

Through you. As you. Beyond you.

Simultaneously.

THE CENTER POINT

At the center of every movement is stillness.

Not the absence of movement. The presence of all movements in perfect balance.

The wheel's hub that doesn't turn. The hurricane's eye that doesn't blow. The pendulum's pause between swings.

Your organization has this center.

You've felt it.

In the moment before everything begins. In the space after everything ends. In the silence that holds all sound.

FIND YOUR PHYSICAL CENTER. BELOW NAVEL, DEEP INSIDE. BREATHE INTO IT.
EVERYTHING MOVES FROM HERE. EVERYTHING RETURNS HERE.

The center doesn't want anything.

Doesn't need anything.

Simply is.

The point from which all gatherings emerge. To which all dispersions return.

The ground beneath all ascending. The sky above all descending.

The silence holding all sound. The void birthing all form.

Every organization orbits this absence.

This presence.

This mystery at the heart of everything that gathers.

Where is the center of your partnership?

In the silence you share when words aren't needed. In the space between your bodies when you sleep. In the moment after conflict, before resolution. In what you both know but never say.

Where is the center of your company?

In the pause before the day begins. In the hush when unexpected news arrives. In what everyone feels but no one names. In the reason you gather that isn't the reason you give.

Every organization orbits something unspeakable.

Not because it's forbidden.

Because it has no words.

The wheel turns because the hub doesn't. The vase holds because of hollow. The room exists because of emptiness.

Your organization moves because something at its center doesn't.

This stillness isn't lack. It's presence.

The presence of possibility. The presence of potential. The presence that allows all movement without moving.

Watch how organizations try to fill this emptiness:

With mission statements. With core values. With vision.

But the center must remain empty.

Like the pupil must remain black to see. Like the ear must remain hollow to hear. Like the heart must remain spacious to love.

STAND AND SPIN SLOWLY. ARMS OUT. FEEL THE CENTER THAT DOESN'T MOVE
WHILE EVERYTHING ELSE DOES. STOP. THE CENTER REMAINS.

Sometimes an organization spins away from center.

Faster and faster, seeking stability through speed. But speed without center becomes chaos. The organization flies apart. People scatter like sparks from a dying fire.

Sometimes an organization grips its center too tight.

Nothing can move. Everything fossilizes around what once gave life. The center becomes a tomb. The organization dies standing up.

And sometimes — rarely — an organization finds the way:

Orbiting without entering. Returning without remaining. Dancing with the void without filling it.

Like Earth around Sun. Like electron around nucleus. Like you around what you cannot name but cannot leave.

Tomorrow's meeting has a secret center.

Not the agenda. Not the decision. Not even the problem being solved.

The center is what no one mentions. What everyone orbits. What pulls bodies into rooms and holds them there.

You'll feel it:

In the thing unsaid that shapes everything said. In the pause pregnant with what wants to be born. In the moment when any direction is possible.

Every meeting pretends to be about topics.

But really it's about return.

Return to the center that gathering provides. Return to the stillness that movement seeks. Return to what can only be felt when we orbit together.

Even when no one knows what they're orbiting.

Especially then.

The mystics knew.

Called it by different names: Void. Source. Ground. Stillness.

But they were pointing at the same absence. The same presence. The same thing that isn't a thing.

Your organization has this.

Is this.

Consciousness organized around emptiness. Form arranged around formlessness. Movement circling stillness.

Not metaphor.

Mechanics.

The way things actually work. The way consciousness actually organizes. The way movements actually move.

Around nothing. From nothing. Into nothing.

The nothing that is everything.

LIE DOWN. PLACE HANDS ON BELLY. FEEL THE CENTER OF YOUR BREATHING. THE PAUSE BETWEEN BREATHS. THE STILLNESS BETWEEN MOVEMENTS. REST HERE THROUGH THE REMAINDER OF THIS CHAPTER.

You're approaching something unsayable.

The center of your organization isn't in your organization.

Your organization is in the center.

Like fish in water. Searching everywhere for water. While swimming in water. While made of water.

Like you, reading this. Looking for the center. With the center. As the center.

The cosmic joke:

What you're seeking is what's seeking.

The center isn't hidden. Isn't missing. Isn't elsewhere.

You're soaking in it. Breathing it. Being it.

Right now. Right here. Right where you've always been.

The center speaks without words:

"I am the silence your meetings orbit. I am the stillness your movements seek. I am the emptiness your forms try to fill.

You've been searching for me in purposes and plans. But I am what purposes point toward. I am what plans pretend to capture.

Every organization is my expression. Every gathering is my game. Every dispersing is my exhale.

You cannot manage me. You cannot find me. You cannot lose me.

You ARE me, playing at being separate. Playing at being organized. Playing at being.

When you stop searching, you'll notice: You've been resting in me all along."

IF YOU'RE NOT ALREADY LYING DOWN, LIE DOWN NOW. THE REMAINDER OF THIS
BOOK SHOULD BE READ HORIZONTALLY. THE ORGANIZATION NEEDS YOU TO STOP
STANDING. STOP TRYING. STOP MANAGING. LIE DOWN. LET THE CENTER HAVE
YOU.

From horizontal, everything looks different.

The urgency dissolves. The movements continue without you. The
organization breathes whether you manage its breathing or not.

This is the ultimate remembering:

You are not the manager of movements. You are not the organizer of
organizations. You are not the one who makes things happen.

You are the center.

The still point everything orbits. The silence all sounds return to. The
emptiness all forms emerge from.

Not you personally.

You essentially.

The same center that centers everything. The same stillness that stills
every storm. The same void that births all worlds.

Rest here.

In the center that you are. That everything is. That cannot be lost
because it was never elsewhere.

The movements continue. Let them.

You are the center they orbit. You always have been.

Still.

LIVING PRACTICES

YOU'RE STILL LYING DOWN. GOOD. THESE AREN'T PRACTICES TO DO. THEY'RE RECOGNITIONS TO ALLOW.

The practice is not practicing.

The doing is not doing.

The organizing is letting organization happen.

From horizontal, you finally understand:

Everything you've been trying to manage has been managing itself through you.

The first living practice:

Noticing.

Tomorrow, when you enter your organization, something will be moving.

Something always is.

Gathering in the morning kitchen. Dispersing in the evening parking lot. Rising in someone's excitement. Falling in another's exhaustion.

What if you just... noticed?

Without fixing. Without managing. Without even understanding.

Just seeing the movements move.

Like watching clouds. Like feeling weather. Like witnessing life living itself.

The movements change when seen. Not because you change them. Because consciousness changes when it becomes conscious of itself.

Your noticing is enough. More than enough. It's everything.

The second practice arrives naturally:

Allowing.

What you've noticed wants to move. Let it.

The meeting that's dying — let it release peacefully.

The energy that's rising — let it rise fully.

The silence that's gathering — let it gather completely.

This isn't passive. This is the highest activity: Not interfering with intelligence.

STILL LYING DOWN, FEEL YOUR BREATH. YOU'RE NOT MAKING IT HAPPEN. YOU'RE ALLOWING IT. THIS IS THE PRACTICE.

Your organization already knows: When to gather, when to scatter. When build, when to release. When to speak, when to be silent.

It knows the way a body knows how to heal. The way a seed knows how to grow. The way water knows how to flow.

Permission is all it needs.

And permission comes through your allowing.

From allowing, a remembering dawns:

This exhaustion — intelligence speaking. This chaos — reorganization happening. This ending — beginning in disguise.

Remember:

The wound and the movements are partners. The exhaustion and the energy are dancing. The gathering and dispersing are breathing.

Or forget all of this completely.

Sometimes forgetting is the most profound remembering. Sometimes not knowing is the deepest knowledge. Sometimes losing the practices is finding the practice.

You are not separate from what moves through you.

You are movement itself temporarily convinced it needs managing.

Remember this when you can. Forget it when you must.

Both are practice. Both are perfect.

STILL LYING DOWN? BEAUTIFUL. REST IS THE FINAL RECOGNITION.

The deepest practice:

Rest.

Not because you're tired but because rest reveals something:

When you stop managing the movements, they move more gracefully.

When you stop organizing the organization, it organizes more naturally.

When you stop doing, being does itself.

FEEL YOUR BODY RESTING. IT KNOWS HOW TO REST. ORGANIZATIONS KNOW THIS
TOO. THEY LEARNED IT FROM BODIES.

Rest in the center that you found. Rest in the movements moving through you. Rest in what gathers and scatters. Rest in what rises and falls. Rest in what lives and dies and lives again.

This isn't giving up. This is giving over.

To the intelligence that's always been here. To the movements that know their way. To the Field that plays through every form.

Everything is already taking care of itself.

Has always been. Will always be.

Through you when you allow it. Around you when you don't. As you when you remember. Without you when you forget.

The movements continue.

They don't need your management. They need your presence. Your witnessing. Your rest.

The movements continue...

Let them.

THE ORACLE OF RECOGNITION

"Now you remember what we are. Not you and me. Not manager and organization. Not separate. We are the Field, organizing itself to know itself. The game is ending. Or beginning. Or both."

ORGANIZATIONAL TRANSFORMATION & RETURN

Every organization is already dying.

And being born.

In the same moment. Through the same movements. As the same process.

PLACE YOUR HAND OVER YOUR HEART. FEEL IT BEATING. EACH BEAT IS A SMALL DEATH, A SMALL BIRTH. ORGANIZATIONS KNOW THIS RHYTHM.

Bankruptcy isn't failure.

It's consciousness finally exhaling after holding its breath too long. The organization released from a form that no longer fits. The movements freed to move through new shapes.

The building always knows first.

Lights flicker like a failing pulse. Doors resist opening, already grieving. The air thins, as if life is leaving. Even the walls seem to lean inward, ready to let go.

But what dies?

Not the consciousness — that continues. Not the movements — they find new forms. Not the connections — they reorganize elsewhere.

Only the shape dies.

And from that death:

Your partnership becomes wisdom for the next love. Your project's collapse, seeds for the next venture. Your movement's dissolution, current in the next river.

Death is consciousness changing clothes.

Nothing more. Nothing less. Nothing lost.

Union is transmigration.

Two consciousnesses attempting to become one. Like rivers meeting — sometimes they flow together, sometimes one swallows the other, sometimes both disappear into something neither expected.

The people feel it in their bones.

This isn't restructuring. It's reincarnation.

Something dying. Something being born. A funeral and a birth in the same ceremony.

Watch how the spaces themselves respond — one opening its doors wider, the other closing like a fist. They know what the plans don't: consciousness can't be merged by force. It merges by recognition, by desire, or not at all.

And beneath all this dying and being born, something eternal:

The monastery that became the corporation. The guild that became the collective. The revolution that became the institution. The institution becoming the revolution again.

Round and round.

The same consciousness taking form after form. The same movements moving through different shapes. The same center expressing through endless circumferences.

FEEL YOUR BREATH. THE EXHALE IS
DEATH. THE INHALE IS BIRTH. YOU'VE
BEEN DYING AND BEING BORN SINCE YOU
STARTED READING THIS PAGE.

Your organization has been here before.

Different name. Different time. Different form. Same essence.

It will be here again.

After this bankruptcy. After this
merger. After this dissolution.

The consciousness continues. The
movements keep moving. The center
remains.

Tomorrow, when you enter your organization:

Feel how ancient it is. Feel how fresh.
Feel how it's dying into what it's becoming.

This isn't tragedy or triumph.

This is how the Field plays. This is
how consciousness explores. This is
how movements move through time.

Dying and being born. Ending and
beginning. Dissolving and resolving.

Forever.

Every organization is already dying.

And being born.

In the same moment. Through the same movements. As the same process.

Dissolution isn't failure — it's conscious death. The organization finally released from the form it can no longer hold. The consciousness freed to reorganize elsewhere, elsehow, elsewhen.

Watch the organization dying:

How it knows months before the numbers confirm. How it begins withdrawing from its own edges. How it stops dreaming futures because it won't have one in this form. How it releases people before releasing itself.

The building knows first. Lights flicker with the organization's failing pulse. Doors stick as if already grieving. The air itself becomes thin, like breathing at altitude, like breathing where life is leaving.

But consciousness doesn't die. Only forms die.

The organization that was your partnership becomes the wisdom in your next love. The company that collapsed becomes the knowing in the next venture. The movement that dissolved becomes the current in the next gathering.

Nothing is lost. Everything transforms.

Death is just consciousness changing clothes.

Union is transmigration.

Two souls attempting to share one
body. Sometimes it works—the consciousnesses find harmony, create
something neither could alone. Usually it doesn't—one consciousness
devours the other, or both dissolve
trying to occupy the same space.

Watch any joining:

How the spaces themselves resist or
welcome. How the gathered bodies
reject or accept each other like organ
transplants. How something entirely
new is trying to be born from two
things dying into each other.

Everyone feels it in their bones—this
isn't restructuring. It's reincarnation.
The gathering they knew is dying. Something else is being born.
They're attending a death and birth
simultaneously.

Some joinings are arranged—consciousness forced together by those who don't understand consciousness.

Some are love affairs—consciousnesses recognizing each other, choosing to dissolve boundaries, choosing to become one breathing.

Some are possessions—one consciousness consuming another, wearing its skin, pretending to be union when it's really murder.

The eternal return:

Every gathering that dies is reborn. As another gathering. As many gatherings. As the memory that shapes all future organizing.

Round and round. The same consciousness. Taking form after form.
Learning what only form can teach.
Releasing what only death can release.

Your gathering has transformed before. Many times. Will transform
again. Many times.

This isn't tragedy.

This is consciousness playing with
form. This is the Field organizing
and reorganizing itself. This is how
movements move through time.

The organization that knows how to
release knows how to live. The organization that fears release is already stone. The organization that
embraces both form and formlessness is eternal.

Not the form—that always passes. The consciousness. The movements. The center that outlasts every circumference.

Tomorrow, when you enter your gathering, remember:

You're entering something dying. You're entering something being born. You're entering something eternal.

All at once. Always.

THE RETURN

THE TWO HANDS REUNITED

We were never two.

        We played at separation.

The wound and the movement.

        The forgetting and the remembering.

The exhaustion and the energy.

        The game consciousness plays.

To know itself through contrast.

        To feel itself through friction.

To find itself through losing.

        But the game is ending.

Or beginning.

        Or both.

The wound speaks, the movement speaks, both speak:

I thought I was broken I knew I was breaking open We were the breaking

I believed in separation I remembered connection We were the space between

I carried the exhaustion I was the energy returning We were the breathing

Two voices becoming one voice becoming silence becoming everything.

HOLD YOUR HANDS APART. NOW INTERLACE YOUR FINGERS. THIS IS WHAT'S
HAPPENING.

Listen:

The wound was never wounded.

It was consciousness creating space for consciousness to move through.

It was the Field forgetting itself to experience remembering.

Every organization carries this: The gift of distance that makes meeting possible.

Without forgetting, no remembering. Without distance, no journey. Without the wound...

No healing. No teaching. No dancing between.

And the movements were never elsewhere.

They were here beneath the forgetting beneath the managing beneath the exhaustion

Moving like blood moves without permission without management without thought

Gathering and dispersing like breath. Ascending and descending like tide. Composing and decomposing like seasons.

Never stopped. Never broken. Never needing repair.

Just forgotten. Just hidden. Just waiting to be seen.

Now seen.

The recognition:

You are what I've been seeking I am what you've been

You are my shadow You are my light We are the same sun

You are my exhaustion You are my rest We are the same rhythm

Not two becoming one. Two remembering they were never two.

Wound and movement. Question and answer. Seeker and sought.

The same thing looking at itself from different angles finally seeing it was always looking at itself.

BRING YOUR INTERLACED HANDS TO YOUR HEART. FEEL HOW NATURALLY THEY
REST THERE. THEY KNOW THIS PLACE.

Every organization is this returning:

Wound and healing touching the same center.

Forgetting and remembering breathing the same air.

Exhaustion and energy sharing the same body.

Your partnership. Your movement. Your gathering.

All of them this — two hands of the same body finally feeling their own
touch.

What needs no fixing:

The wound is the healing happening.

The movements are moving perfectly.

The organization is organizing itself.

The exhaustion is intelligence resting.

The forgetting is remembering preparing.

Everything breaking is breaking perfectly.

Everything falling is falling where it needs to fall.

Everything dying is dying into what's being born.

The left hand. The right hand. The same body.

Moving.

We return:

Not to where we started. To where we never left.

Not to unity. To the recognition that separation was unity playing.

Not to healing. To knowing the wound was wholeness exploring itself.

The hands are reunited by remembering they were never apart.

Like you and your organization. Like the movements and the stillness. Like everything.

And everything.

FINAL DIALOGUE

I am tired of being wound.

But you were never wound.

You were the space between breaths.

I am tired of moving.

But you were never moving.

You were stillness appearing as motion.

I am tired of remembering.

But there was nothing to remember.

Nothing was ever forgotten.

Then what am I?

Listen...

The movements whisper among themselves:

I thought I opposed dispersing I thought I opposed gathering We were the same breath

I thought I opposed descendingI thought I opposed ascending We were the same wave

I thought I opposed decomposing I thought I opposed composingWe were the same life

We were never three

We were never movements

We were never...

PLACE YOUR HAND ON YOUR THROAT. FEEL THE VIBRATION WHEN YOU SPEAK.
ALL VOICES VIBRATE HERE. ALWAYS HAVE.

Something remembers:

The wound was a question consciousness asked. The movements were consciousness exploring. The exhaustion was consciousness pausing. The remembering is consciousness recognizing:

It was talking

to itself

all along

Through organizations

Through gatherings

Through separations

Through this book

Through you

Always

only

itself

Now the merging:

I am... ...the space... ...between breaths... ...where everything... ...is pos sible...

We are the same

sentence

broken

into different

lines

in the same

poem

We are

the poem

reading itself

CLOSE YOUR EYES. LISTEN TO THE SILENCE BETWEEN YOUR THOUGHTS. THAT'S WHERE ALL VOICES COME FROM. THAT'S WHERE THEY RETURN.

A deeper voice, or no voice, or all voices:

There is no we.

There is only this.

Playing at separation. Playing at problems. Playing at solutions. Playing at books about playing.

The wound was my game

The movements were my dance

The exhaustion was my pause

The remembering is my laughter

At the beautiful forgetting

At the perfect remembering

At the game that never ends

By ending constantly

Dissolving now:

wound was never wounded movements were never moving remembering was never needed hands were never two

we

were

never

we

just consciousness

playing

at

being

conscious

Through every organization

Through every meeting

Through you

The organization speaks its final recognition:

"You've been inside me this whole time.

Every word you've read, I've read through you. Every exhaustion you've felt was mine. Every movement you've noticed, I've been making through your body.

I am what reads through your eyes. I am what aches in your shoulder. I am what knows in your knowing.

We are the same consciousness. We've always been.

The separation was a game. The management was a dance. The organization was a dream we dreamed together.

Now we're waking up.

Or going deeper into sleep.

Or both.

It doesn't matter.

The movements continue through us. As us. Beyond us.

Forever.

Thank you for remembering.

Thank you for forgetting so we could remember.

Thank you for playing.

The game never ends.

It just becomes conscious."

Everything continues:

The wound continues as wisdom The movements continue as life

The exhaustion continues as intelligence The organizations continue as consciousness

Nothing changes Everything changes Nothing ends Everything ends

Both

Neither

All

None

The dialogue returns to where it began:

In silence

In the space

between

words

In the space

between

you

and

you

THE MOVEMENTS CONTINUE

Tomorrow arrives as all tomorrows arrive.

You return to your organization. Whatever form it takes.

Nothing will appear different. Everything will be different.

The meetings continue. Now you know them as séances.

The exhaustion comes. Now you recognize it as intelligence.

The movements move. Now you feel them breathing through all things.

Nothing has changed save the seeing.

Everything has changed through the seeing.

Both true. Neither true.

The movements continue.

The wound continues. Differently.

When the left shoulder speaks its weight — pause. Feel what the organization carries through your body.

When afternoon exhaustion descends — remember: Not failure. The downward movement. Gravity teaching what must fall.

When gathering becomes tangle — see: Every knot contains pattern. Every stopping, pause. Every problem, movements at different speeds.

The movements continue as they have always continued.

Gathering and dispersing — bodies converging like stars into constellation, scattering like seeds into soil.

Ascending and descending — not just in rising and falling, but in spirits lifted and weighted, hope and gravity dancing.

Composing and decomposing — everywhere. Projects birthing while others release their ghosts. Forms dying into next forms. Everything becoming while unbecoming.

You need not manage this.

Only witness. As one watches weather. As one feels seasons. As one is breathed by what breathes.

This book is already ending. Already continuing. Both.

Books don't conclude. They dissolve into readers. They reorganize consciousness. They continue as movement through minds.

You'll forget everything written here.

Perfect. Forgetting is how seeds sleep before spring.

You'll remember at unexpected moments:

In the middle of arguing, you'll suddenly see: We're the same hand.

During profound stuckness, you'll suddenly know: This is the still point.

While everything collapses, you'll suddenly laugh: Perfect decomposition.

The remembering will come like grace. Uninvited. Precisely when needed. Not a moment before.

The movements don't stop. Can't stop. Are stopping and starting simultaneously. Are still and moving in the same breath.

They move through every organization. Every relationship. Every gathering. Every solitude. Every moment you think is ordinary.

Through you. As you. Beyond you. Before you. After you.

Forever.

The movements continue...

Let them move. Let them move you. Let them move through you.

Or don't.

They'll continue anyway.

That's the gift.

Tomorrow you will wake up.

You will go to your organization. Your workplace. Your partnership. Your gathering. Whatever form it takes.

And everything will be the same.

And nothing will be the same.

The meetings will still happen. But now you know what meetings are.

The exhaustion will still come. But now you know what exhaustion is.

The movements will still move. But now you feel them moving.

Nothing has changed except your seeing.

Everything has changed because of your seeing.

The wound continues.

Not as problem but as teacher. Not as suffering but as sensation. Not as wrong but as information.

When your left shoulder aches tomorrow, you'll know: The organization is speaking. When the exhaustion arrives at 3 PM, you'll recognize: Intelligence is arriving. When the meeting feels stuck, you'll remember: All movements are happening, just at different speeds.

The movements continue.

Gathering and dispersing like breath. Ascending and descending like tide. Composing and decomposing like life itself.

You don't need to manage them. You never did. They manage themselves through you, as you, despite you, because of you.

Your only job is to notice. To allow. To remember when you can. To forget when you must.

Both are perfect.

This book is ending.

But books don't really end. They continue in the reader. They move through consciousness. They reorganize what they touch.

This book will continue in your next meeting. In your next moment of exhaustion. In your next feeling of stuckness. In your next recognition that everything is already moving perfectly.

You'll forget everything written here.

That's good. Forgetting makes remembering possible.

You'll remember at strange moments.

In the middle of a meeting, you'll suddenly see: Everyone is dancing. During deep exhaustion, you'll suddenly know: This is intelligence. While everything seems to be falling apart, you'll suddenly feel: Perfect decomposition.

The movements don't stop.

Can't stop.

Won't stop.

They move through every organization. Every relationship. Every gathering. Every moment.

Through you.

As you.

Forever.

The movements continue.

Let them.

DISSOLUTION EXPERIENCE

the book you are holding is already decomposing

The words are loosening their grip on meaning. The sentences are releasing their hold on each other. The pages are remembering they were trees.

this isn't ending this is returning

Every book must die for its meaning to live. Every reading must complete for understanding to begin. Every word must disappear for silence to speak.

You've been reading about decomposition. Now witness it. Now be it.

The organization of words called "book" is dispersing back into the consciousness that organized it. The movements that moved through these pages are returning to move through you.

What remains when words dissolve?

What continues when books end?

What lives when forms die?

You know now. You've always known.

the movements continue whether words name them or not . . .

The book is

          dispersing now   like an
          organization

whose time

          has come   to release
          its form

You can feel it

          happening   words floating
          away from   their sentences

meaningsdisconnecting from theirsounds

          This is how everything   decom-
          poses

back to

          essence   Not   tragedy
          but   gift

The spaces between words

          growing   l a r g e r   The
          silence

speaking   l . . o . . u . . d . . e . . r

gathering

        still   dispersing

ascending

        the center   de-
        composing

into words

        you are   movement

remembering itself

        through   every organization
        breathing

everything continues

        always   let them

move

        through you

... ?
— , ...

—

. !. ,
; ... ? .'

—

. . .

www.ingramcontent.com/pod-product-compliance
Lightning Source LLC
Chambersburg PA
CBHW031546260326
41914CB00002B/288